WORLD
HISTORY SERIES ■ ■ ■

The Watts Riot

Titles in the World History Series

The Age of Augustus
The Age of Feudalism
The Age of Pericles
The American Frontier
The American Revolution
Ancient Greece
The Ancient Near East
Architecture
Aztec Civilization
The Black Death
The Byzantine Empire
Caesar's Conquest of Gaul
The California Gold Rush
The Chinese Cultural
    Revolution
The Conquest of Mexico
The Crusades
The Cuban Missile Crisis
The Cuban Revolution
The Early Middle Ages
Egypt of the Pharaohs
Elizabethan England
The End of the Cold War
The French and Indian War
The French Revolution
The Glorious Revolution
The Great Depression
Greek and Roman Theater

The History of Slavery
Hitler's Reich
The Hundred Years' War
The Inquisition
The Italian Renaissance
The Late Middle Ages
The Lewis and Clark
    Expedition
The Mexican Revolution
The Mexican War of
    Independence
Modern Japan
The Punic Wars
The Reformation
The Relocation of the
    North American Indian
The Roman Empire
The Roman Republic
The Russian Revolution
The Scientific Revolution
The Spread of Islam
Traditional Africa
Traditional Japan
The Travels of Marco Polo
Twentieth Century Science
The Wars of the Roses
The Watts Riot
Women's Suffrage

WORLD
HISTORY SERIES ■ ■ ■

The Watts Riot

by
Liza N. Burby

Lucent Books, P.O. Box 289011, San Diego, CA 92198-9011

Library of Congress Cataloging-in-Publication Data

Burby, Liza N.
   The Watts riot / by Liza N. Burby.
      p.   cm. — (World history series)
   Includes bibliographical references and index.
   Summary: Describes the 1965 riot in the black neighborhood of Watts that shook Los Angeles and the nation.
   ISBN 1-56006-300-9 (alk. paper)
   1. Watts Riot, Los Angeles, Calif., 1965—Juvenile literature.
2. Los Angeles (Calif.)—Race relations—Juvenile literature.
3. Afro-Americans—California—Los Angeles—Social conditions—Juvenile literature. 4. Afro-Americans—Civil rights—
California—Los Angeles. [1. Watts Riot, Los Angeles, Calif.,
1965. 2. Afro-Americans—Civil rights. 3. Afro-Americans—
Social conditions. 4. Race relations.] I. Title. II. Series.
F869.L89.N4   1997
979.4'94—dc21   96-54585
                                                    CIP
                                                     AC

Always use the subjects in brackets

973.922

Contents

Foreword

Each year on the first day of school, nearly every history teacher faces the task of explaining why his or her students should study history. One logical answer to this question is that exploring what happened in our past explains how the things we often take for granted—our customs, ideas, and institutions—came to be. As statesman and historian Winston Churchill put it, "Every nation or group of nations has its own tale to tell. Knowledge of the trials and struggles is necessary to all who would comprehend the problems, perils, challenges, and opportunities which confront us today." Thus, a study of history puts modern ideas and institutions in perspective. For example, though the founders of the United States were talented and creative thinkers, they clearly did not invent the concept of democracy. Instead, they adapted some democratic ideas that had originated in ancient Greece and with which the Romans, the British, and others had experimented. An exploration of these cultures, then, reveals their very real connection to us through institutions that continue to shape our daily lives.

Another reason often given for studying history is the idea that lessons exist in the past from which contemporary societies can benefit and learn. This idea, although controversial, has always been an intriguing one for historians. Those that agree that society can benefit from the past often quote philosopher George Santayana's famous statement, "Those who cannot remember the past are condemned to repeat it." Historians who ascribe to Santayana's philosophy believe that, for example, studying the events that led up to the major world wars or other significant historical events would allow society to chart a different and more favorable course in the future.

Just as difficult as convincing students to realize the importance of studying history is the search for useful and interesting supplementary materials that present historical events in a context that can be easily understood. The volumes in Lucent Books' World History Series attempt to present a broad, balanced, and penetrating view of the march of history. Ancient Egypt's important wars and rulers, for example, are presented against the rich and colorful backdrop of Egyptian religious, social, and cultural developments. The series engages the reader by enhancing historical events with these cultural contexts. For example, in *Ancient Greece*, the text covers the role of women in that society. Slavery is discussed in *The Roman Empire*, as well as how slaves earned their freedom. The numerous and varied aspects of everyday life in these and other societies are explored in each volume of the series. Additionally, the series covers the major political, cultural, and philosophical ideas as the torch of civilization is passed from ancient Mesopotamia and Egypt, through Greece, Rome, Medieval Europe, and other world cultures, to the modern day.

The material in the series is formatted in a thorough, precise, and organized manner. Each volume offers the reader a comprehensive and clearly written overview of an important historical event or period. The topic under discussion is placed in a broad historical context. For example, *The Italian Renaissance* begins with a discussion of the High Middle Ages and the loss of central control that allowed certain Italian cities to develop artistically. The book ends by looking forward to the Reformation and interpreting the societal changes that grew out of the Renaissance. Thus, students are not only involved in an historical era, but also enveloped by the events leading up to that era and the events following it.

One important and unique feature in the World History Series is the primary and secondary source quotations that richly supplement each volume. These quotes are useful in a number of ways. First, they allow students access to sources they would not normally be exposed to because of the difficulty and obscurity of the original source. The quotations range from interesting anecdotes to farsighted cultural perspectives and are drawn from historical witnesses both past and present. Second, the quotes demonstrate how and where historians themselves derive their information on the past as they strive to reach a consensus on historical events. Lastly, all of the quotes are footnoted, familiarizing students with the citation process and allowing them to verify quotes and/or look up the original source if the quote piques their interest.

Finally, the books in the World History Series provide a detailed launching point for further research. Each book contains a bibliography specifically geared toward student research. A second, annotated bibliography introduces students to all the sources the author consulted when compiling the book. A chronology of important dates gives students an overview, at a glance, of the topic covered. Where applicable, a glossary of terms is included.

In short, the series is designed not only to acquaint readers with the basics of history, but also to make them aware that their lives are a part of an ongoing human saga. Perhaps they will then come to the same realization as famed historian Arnold Toynbee. In his monumental work, *A Study of History*, he wrote about becoming aware of history flowing through him in a mighty current, and of his own life "welling like a wave in the flow of this vast tide."

Important Dates in the History of the Watts Riot

1895	1900	1905	1910	1915	1920	1925	1930	1935	1940

1896
U.S. Supreme Court in *Plessy v. Ferguson* rejects opportunity to declare separate-but-equal or Jim Crow laws illegal; it will be more than sixty years before the laws of this type, which gave official backing to racial segregation, are declared unconstitutional.

May 17, 1954
U.S. Supreme Court rules on *Brown v. Board of Education of Topeka*. Most people believe the civil rights movement began, with this decision, which outlawed segregation in public schools.

May 31, 1955
Brown II gives states authority to order school desegregation.

December 1, 1955
Rosa Parks is arrested for refusing to give up her bus seat to a white man in Montgomery, Alabama.

December 5, 1955 to December 21, 1956
Montgomery bus boycott.

November 13, 1956
Supreme Court ruling outlaws segregation on buses.

1960
Sit-ins and boycotts all over the South and in some northern cities.

1962
U.S. Commission on Civil Rights sends team to Watts to investigate claims of police brutality against blacks.

1963
California legislature enacts a fair housing law: Proposition 14 or the Rumford Act.

June 19, 1963
President John F. Kennedy introduces civil rights bill to Congress.

August 28, 1963
Hundreds of thousands of civil rights supporters participate in the March on Washington; leaders meet with President Kennedy to stress the need to pass the Civil Rights Act.

1964
Two Watts teenagers prepare a report, "Watts: Its Problems and Possible Solutions," indicating the level of poverty in the ghetto.

Summer 1964
Riots break out in Harlem and Rochester, New York, Newark, New Jersey, Chicago, and Philadelphia.

July 2, 1964
Passage of the Civil Rights Act, which declares racial segregation illegal and mandates affirmative action in hiring.

November 4, 1964
The California Real Estate Association protests Proposition 14 and it is overturned.

March 21, 1965
March on Selma, Alabama, to gain support for passage of voting rights legislation.

August 6, 1965
Passage of the Voting Rights Act.

Wednesday, August 11, 1965
Marquette, Ronald, and Rena Frye, and Joyce Ann Gaines are arrested in Watts and the Watts riot begins.

Thursday, August 12, 1965
Violence increases; Los Angeles County Human Relations Commission calls a meeting with police personnel in Athens Park; Police Chief William H. Parker alerts the National Guard.

Friday, August 13, 1965
The worst day of the riot: the National Guard arrives, the first deaths occur; looting begins in earnest.

Saturday, August 14, 1965
Governor Edmund Brown declares a curfew.

Sunday, August 15, 1965
Looting and burning continue.

Monday, August 16, 1965
The curfew and presence of the National Guard bring the riot to an end.

Tuesday, August 17, 1965
Governor Brown ends curfew.

Wednesday, August 18, 1965
The National Guard begins to withdraw. Martin Luther King Jr. visits Watts and is sent away by rioters.

August 24, 1965
Governor Brown appoints the McCone Commission to investigate causes of Watts riot and gives them one hundred days to respond.

December 6, 1965
McCone Commission releases its report: "Violence in the City—An End or a Beginning?"

1966–1967
Riots in 150 cities; the worst riot breaks out in Detroit.

1968
Passage of Civil Rights Act, makes race discrimination in housing illegal.

April 29, 1992
Another riot erupts in Watts, the worst in U.S. history.

August 11, 1995
Watts acknowledges the thirtieth anniversary of the 1965 riot.

Image and Reality

On a sultry night in August 1965, gunshots popped and fires sizzled in the Watts section of the City of Angels, Los Angeles, California, engulfing 22,000 participants in a riot that lasted six days. When the smoke finally cleared in the ghetto, 34 people were dead, 1,032 were injured, and 3,952 men and women had been arrested. There was extensive property damage as well. A total of 201 buildings had been destroyed by fire and 536 buildings had been damaged or looted. The total cost of property damage was estimated at $40 million.

The arrest of a young African-American man on drunken driving charges had ignited what became the symbol of racial conflict in the United States: the Watts riot. The violence of August 11 through 16 did more than impact the two and one-half square miles of the Watts community and the more than forty-six square miles of South Central Los Angeles to which the violence spread. This revolt, as some of the black citizens of Watts said they preferred to call it, gained the ghetto national attention. It also brought issues about the plight of black Americans in inner cities into the living rooms of millions of Americans who sat in front of their televisions watching buildings crumble, police beating African-American citizens, and National Guard tanks rolling down the palm tree–lined streets of Watts. At a time when American soldiers—black and white—were fighting in the Vietnam War in Southeast Asia, people were shocked to see a war zone on American soil.

An Explosive Situation

But the Watts riot was not the first in the United States, nor was it to be the last. Just the summer before, small outbursts of violence had occurred in the poor communities populated mostly by African Americans in New York, New Jersey, Illinois, and Pennsylvania. Another 150 riots were to occur in the next two years. But in 1965, Watts was considered the most destructive incident of racial violence in U.S. history. Watts became the defining symbol of the level of violence that might be expected from some poverty-stricken citizens who felt they had no hope of improving their lives. Their targets had been primarily property of anyone who they felt stood in the way of improving their lives, particularly white business owners; special hostility was directed toward the Los Angeles Police Department. Writer James E. Jackson, who was an eyewitness to much of the Watts riot, expressed the

The National Guard patrols the seemingly war-torn streets of Watts during the riot. Many Americans were shocked to see such images of devastation in their own country.

feelings of the rioters when he said: "This was an elemental scream of outrage from a violated people entombed in a prison house of social deprivation and economic impoverishment."[1]

The Unexpected Riot

The riot surprised many Americans who for more than a decade had dedicated themselves to improving the civil rights of African Americans. The civil rights movement had successfully fought to end legally enforced segregation, which had kept black and white people from living together. By using nonviolent methods, civil rights activists were able to achieve changes in laws and customs that had prevented black children from attending the same schools as white children and all black people from sitting beside white people on buses and in restaurants. Another hard-won battle of the civil rights movement had been gaining the rights of all black citizens to vote, so that they could have a voice in the country's decisions. In fact, the Voting Rights Act became law just days before the riot, on August 6, 1965.

More than One Cause of the Riot

When the riot had been subdued, everyone searched for causes. There were many individual theories. However, the Watts riot was the result of a combination of many circumstances, rather than just one cause. Some of these factors are mentioned in this excerpt from "Los Angeles: The Fire This Time," which appeared in Newsweek *magazine less than two weeks after the end of the riot.*

"The trouble in Los Angeles closely followed the pattern of the riots of 1964, and the roots were just as easy to isolate: the men on the dole, the kids out of school and out of work, the broken families and blighted homes, the smoldering resentment of the cops born long before the inevitable pamphleteering nationalists turned up with their predictable 'police brutality' leaflets. Los Angeles has long prided itself on its cool racial climate—but it has dawdled over proposals to set up a city human-relations commission to assure a continuing black and white dialogue. Police Chief William Parker, the city's tough top cop, was sure the spark was lit indirectly by civil-rights militants: 'You cannot tell people to disobey the law and not expect them to have a disrespect for the law. You cannot keep telling them that they are being abused and mistreated without expecting them to react.' But the answers lay deeper: the kindling had collected for years, now nothing more than an uncommonly hot night and a routine traffic arrest set it aflame."

But the rage that had erupted in Los Angeles proved to be a turning point in the movement. It sent a clear message to civil rights activists that despite the new laws, there were segregated neighborhoods in northern and western cities where the movement had not made an impact. The nation was used to reading and hearing about the peaceful demonstrations in the southern cities by blacks and their white supporters. But the riot in the Watts section of Los Angeles, a West Coast city whose black population was considered to be the most prosperous in the country, came without warning. A reporter in a 1965 *Ebony* article said, "The outbreak stunned the nation. Harlem or Chicago, yes; Birmingham, maybe, but never, never Los Angeles. It was the wrong time and the wrong place."[2] But as in other inner cities, the mostly African-American population in Watts lived in poverty with no immediate prospects of relief.

The people of Watts were not surprised that their neighbors rioted. To look at the history of Watts and the conditions for inner-city residents throughout the country is to understand that the fires that raged in Watts that summer had been kindled generations before. Poverty, inadequate housing, and widespread unemployment sucked the life out of many Watts residents, leaving them angry and despairing. The violence was also fueled by the perception of young black people of Watts that there was one enemy: the white police officer of the Los Angeles Police Department. Complaints by youths that police officers beat and harassed them were so numerous that in 1962 a California civil rights advisory committee had investigated some of the charges. But the committee had found no evidence to support the charges, and police relations with Watts residents continued as before. This added to the anger of the South Central Los Angeles residents until their hostility exploded on August 11

The Watts riot of 1965 was eclipsed in terms of destruction and casualties by a 1992 riot near Watts (pictured).

and raged until it was brought under control by the National Guard on August 16.

When the riot was all over, the people of Watts were left to pick up the pieces. For a while, some public funding was poured into the area. For a while, the city officials focused on the conditions of African Americans in Watts and said they would make improvements. For a while, the nation listened to what African Americans in the ghettos of America had to say. And then it happened again, worse this

The Level of Violence Surprises African Americans

Blacks familiar with conditions in the Watts ghetto were not surprised that a riot erupted. However, many were taken aback at the level of destruction and violence, as indicated in the essay "The Watts Rising," excerpted from A Documentary History of the Negro People in the United States, *edited by Herbert Aptheker. The author of the essay, Roy Wilkins, was executive director of the National Association for the Advancement of Colored People and a leader in the civil rights movement at the time of the riot.*

"The passion of Watts, the rage, the fires, the crackle of gunfire, the looting all took whites by surprise. I was not surprised in the slightest. We had had early warnings the year before in Harlem and elsewhere. Even so, California had blithely passed a statewide proposition rejecting fair housing, an injury that could only make California Negroes feel hopelessly penned in their ghettos. The chief of police in Los Angeles was the sort of fellow who could call Negroes 'monkeys in a zoo.' Mayor Sam Yorty was a law-and-order man—law for the white folks and plenty of orders for everyone else. Given this background the riot was no surprise, but I was not prepared for the sheer scale of the violence: night after night of bloody spasms that turned fifty square miles of the city into a war zone."

Roy Wilkins (far left) of the NAACP commented on the riot.

time, in Detroit in 1967. And in 1992, history came full circle as a riot occurred just outside Watts, lowering the ranking of the 1965 riot to the third worst in U.S. history. The occurrence of the 1992 riot raised questions of whether the status of poor black citizens of the United States had progressed at all in the three decades since Watts—and what, if anything, had been gained by the riots.

But for a time after that long, hot summer, the people of Watts believed they had made an impact. As one resident said during the 1965 riot: "We know this is not the way. We've got sense enough to know that what happened is bad. But at least somebody is listening to us now. Somebody is concerned."[3]

As the Watts community began to rebuild after the destruction, one thing became certain: The civil rights movement had been altered. No longer would black and white activists try to fight for justice for black citizens without also considering how to ensure that the benefits obtained would extend across inner-city borders. In the words of civil rights leader Martin Luther King Jr., "The flames of Watts illuminated more than the Western sky; they cast light on the imperfections in the Civil Rights movement and the tragic shallowness of white racial policy in the explosive ghettos."[4] The 1965 Watts riot came to signify the split between nonviolent and violent protest, permanently changing the course of civil rights in America.

1 A Decade of Progress

Since the nineteenth century, African Americans had lived with restrictions called Jim Crow laws, which ensured the segregation of the races by providing for the establishment of "separate but equal" public facilities. Schools, parks, swimming pools, trains, and even water fountains came in two forms: white and colored.

Particularly in the South, the facilities set aside for African Americans were seldom equal in size or quality to those reserved for whites; but blacks who decided to select the more desirable accommodations were subject to arrest and jailing. This is what happened to Homer Plessy over a hundred years ago when he refused to leave a section of a train marked "whites only." Upon his release from prison, Plessy sued Judge Ferguson, the Louisiana magistrate who had ordered his incarceration.

The case of *Plessy v. Ferguson* was heard by the U.S. Supreme Court in 1896, and the majority upheld the Louisiana judge's action. This ruling had the effect of legalizing one of the main mechanisms for enforcing segregation, the Jim Crow laws. These laws were supposed to allow blacks the same quality of life as whites, as long as the two races lived separately from each

Protesters in 1963 demand an end to Jim Crow laws, which denied black people the same rights and advantages that whites enjoyed.

A Wake-Up Call

Watts became a wake-up call to the civil rights leaders: It was not enough to work for social change in the South; they needed to protest for the sake of northern blacks, too. In Eyes on the Prize, *Juan Williams discusses this shift in the goals of the movement.*

"Over a period of ten years, the civil rights movement not only dramatically altered the nation, but it also transformed a race. Black people who had lived under oppression for 300 years gained a new sense of dignity and power and a truer sense of citizenship. White people were changed as well—after an unquestioned acceptance of a segregated society, many examined how they treated their black neighbors and went on to accept civil rights as human rights. But changing the hearts and minds of most white people would take more than legislation. After the Selma march, the assassination of Malcolm X [in 1965], and the signing of the Voting Rights Act, a new sense of injustice began to burn in the northern cities."

other. Civil rights activists maintained that the laws did not do this. They pointed out that while every aspect of black and white society was separate, the races were anything but equal. They were uneven economically, educationally, and with respect to access to housing, medical treatment, and recreational activities. In the decade before gunfire erupted in the summer air over Watts, activists formed a movement to change the conditions under which African Americans were forced to live.

The Beginning of the Civil Rights Movement

To most historians, the civil rights movement began on May 17, 1954, when the Supreme Court handed down the *Brown v.*

Board of Education of Topeka decision outlawing segregation in public schools. Until then, black children had been able to attend only schools that were so poorly funded that very few were able to provide education of the same quality that was available to white children. In the *Brown* case, lawyers for the National Association for the Advancement of Colored People (NAACP) also argued that separate-but-equal schools could not exist. Having one set of schools for whites and another for blacks, they said, has a harmful effect on black children's self-esteem, which in turn would make it difficult for them to learn even if the same amount of money were spent on the separate schools. Therefore, the NAACP attorneys stated, as long as segregation existed, the education of black children could not equal that of white children.

Equality in the North?

While before the 1960s segregation of blacks and whites was the law in the South, the North had its own ways of keeping blacks separate from whites. This excerpt from "The Southern Case for School Segregation," written by James Jackson Kilpatrick in 1962, appears in Eyes on the Prize.

"In plain fact, the relationship between white and Negro in the segregated South, in the country and in the city, has been far closer, more honest, less constrained, than such relations generally have been in the integrated North. In Charleston and New Orleans, among many other cities, residential segregation does not exist, for example, as it exists in Detroit or Chicago. In the country, whites and Negroes are farm neighbors. They share the same calamities—the mud, the hail, the weevils—and they minister, in their own unfelt, unspoken way, to one another. Is the relationship one of master and servant, superior or inferior? Down deep, doubtless it is, but I often wonder if this is more wrong to the Negro than the affected, hearty 'equality' encountered in the North."

The Court's decision, handed down by Chief Justice Earl Warren, criticized the separate-but-equal doctrine introduced in the *Plessy* case in 1896 and agreed that its practical effects were harmful to children. The famous ruling reads:

> Does segregation of children in public schools solely on the basis of race, even though the physical facilities and other tangible factors may be equal, deprive children of the minority group of equal education opportunities? We believe it does. . . . To separate them from others of similar age and qualifications solely because of their race generates a feeling of inferiority as to their status in the community that may affect their hearts and minds in a way very unlikely to ever be undone. . . .

We conclude, unanimously, that in the field of public education the doctrine of "separate but equal" has no place. Separate educational facilities are inherently unequal.[5]

The Supreme Court's 1896 doctrine of "separate but equal" was reversed, but only for public education. The Supreme Court in 1954 had called for a major change in American life: African Americans were to be treated as equals in public schools.

Although the *Brown* decision opened the way for equality, it did not include instructions on how the order was to be carried out. Author Juan Williams writes: "Desegregation began almost immediately in Washington, D.C. and Baltimore, but most of the nation waited for the Court to provide specific instructions on how to end school segregation."[6]

A year later, on May 31, 1955, the Supreme Court decided *Brown II*. This ruling gave individual states the authority to order school desegregation. Few schools took the opportunity to desegregate even though *Brown II* ensured that their efforts would not be reversed or punished. This was a message to the people who had been fighting for black civil rights: It was now apparent that the Jim Crow laws would have to be changed one at a time. Author Williams notes some specifics: "When the *Brown* decision was handed down, black people hoped that the foundation on which Jim Crow had built his house would collapse. But in the years that followed, it became clear that the house would have to be dismantled brick by brick—on the buses, at the lunch counters, in the voting booths."[7]

As a result, the civil rights movement began to gather steam, and its focus was on the South, where racial segregation was a way of life. It extended into the smallest details of everyday living. There were separate restaurants and movie theaters, separate hospitals, and even separate public restrooms. Segregation was most keenly felt on the city buses, used by everyone. After paying their fares at the front of the bus, black people had to leave the bus, and reenter at the back door. They were allowed to sit only in the rear of the bus, and they had to give up their seats if white people were left standing. African Americans who did not obey these rules were subject to arrest.

To the Back of the Bus No More

On December 1, 1955, in Montgomery, Alabama, Rosa Parks, tired from a long day at work, refused to give up her seat to a white man. She was arrested and scheduled for trial on the following Monday. The NAACP decided to use this case to stop racial segregation on the buses, and

During the era of segregation, African Americans who did not obey laws proclaimed by signs like this one were subject to arrest.

local activists distributed leaflets asking all black people to boycott, or refuse to use, the city buses on the day of the trial. The boycott worked—African Americans found other transportation that day—but Rosa Parks was found guilty of violating the law. In response, the one-day Montgomery bus boycott of December 5 continued, led by a fiery young clergyman, Martin Luther King Jr. The boycotters warned the city officials that the boycott would not end until segregation on the city buses was overturned. About fifty thousand blacks walked or carpooled to work for twelve months. Sometimes they were met with violence. King's home was firebombed by white protesters. Finally, on November 13, 1956, the Supreme Court outlawed segregation on the buses, and on December 21, 1956, the bus boycott was over. King wrote of this success in his book *Stride Toward Freedom*: "The story of Montgomery is the story of 50,000 Negroes who were willing to substitute tired feet for tired souls and walk the streets of Montgomery until the walls of segregation were finally battered by the forces of justice!"[8]

The Montgomery bus boycott was the first successful mass protest campaign in the South. Its immediate impact was on the hope of African Americans, who saw that by banding together, they could challenge segregation and win. The following year, the tactic was used successfully in Birmingham and Mobile, Alabama, and in Tallahassee, Florida. Bayard Rustin, who had been an aide to King, explains why the boycott had been so important to southern blacks:

> The strong sense of unity and purpose exhibited by the Negro community, the ability of the black citizens to sustain the boycott through month after weary month, their renewed determination in the face of violence all served as an example to the blacks across the South who were thirsting for a movement that could actually threaten basic southern institutions.

The Montgomery boycott was important for other reasons also. It was one of the first protests in which the demands of the black community were comprehensive enough to include both economic rights and human dignity. The Montgomery demands included the abolition of segregated seating patterns, an end to the abusive behavior of white bus drivers, and the hiring of blacks as drivers.[9]

A Nonviolent Movement

After segregated education and transportation had been attacked, black civil rights leaders looked for ways to achieve the desegregation of other aspects of everyday life. King encouraged the philosophy of nonviolent protest. The best approach, he said, was to use passive resistance, which means putting up no physical struggle, even if one is the victim of violence. His belief was that if the movement used violence, it would lose the support of compassionate white people. One nonviolent tactic was the sit-in: People simply sat—for example, at a segregated lunch counter—and refused to budge until their demands were met.

In 1960 a group of students formed the Nashville Student Movement, which became the Student Nonviolent Coordi-

Bayard Rustin, an associate of Martin Luther King Jr., believed the Montgomery bus boycott of 1955 raised the conciousness of both black and white people to the injustice of segregation.

months, the mayor of Nashville gave the order to end segregated seating at lunch counters. The sit-in movement had been a success. By the end of the year, sit-ins had been staged in 112 southern cities, effectively ending segregation in public places in those cities.

Desegregation Becomes the Law

All of the activity of the civil rights movement led to changes in the laws supporting segregation. Much of the time individual protesters were attacked or jailed. But the protests were very much in the public eye, as these activities gained national media attention. In the nine years since the *Brown* decision, America had witnessed intense racial turmoil. Rustin summarizes the gains:

> By 1960, the nation could clearly see the fruits of the civil rights movement. Social and political institutions had in small measure been made to bend. We had captured the attention of the news media and won sympathy from the general public. Legal action continued to produce important breakthroughs. Black people were themselves becoming increasingly more conscious of the civil rights struggle.[10]

However, despite the many successes civil rights protesters had achieved, and the rulings in which the Supreme Court upheld civil rights laws, these laws were not always enforced. Some states were receptive to the laws; others chose to ignore them. Civil rights leaders decided to push for a federal civil rights act, which would outlaw segregation everywhere in the

nating Committee in 1961. They planned to send a group to sit at lunch counters in Tennessee, where African Americans had never been served; they were to try to order something and refuse to move. If arrested, they planned to have other students ready to replace them. If they were served, they would go to the next lunch counter and change that restaurant's policy, too. When all the lunch counters were integrated, they would go to the movie theaters and libraries. The idea spread to other cities. Protesters in Nashville were met with violence and hundreds of students were arrested. But the sit-ins attracted national publicity, and within country, forcing state governments to make the necessary changes.

Eventually their efforts and those of their supporters were successful, and on June 19, 1963, President John F. Kennedy delivered a civil rights bill to Congress that would outlaw all segregation in all public facilities. To encourage passage of the bill, a coalition of civil rights organizations sponsored a march on Washington, D.C., to show how many people demanded this legislation. On August 28, 1963, nearly a quarter of a million people marched. At the time, it was the largest demonstration for human rights in U.S. history. Author Williams writes: "America witnessed an unprecedented spectacle that day. The march brought joy and a sense of possibility to people throughout the nation who perhaps had not understood the civil rights movement before or who had felt threatened by it."[11]

Though many political leaders resisted the Civil Rights Act, it was passed on July 2, 1964. The law, which prohibits discrimination in places of public accommodation like hotels and motels, provided for the establishment of an Equal Employment Opportunity Commission (EEOC), which investigates charges of discrimination. Thereafter, a person who had been turned away from a job on the basis of race, creed, color, religion, or sex could turn to the EEOC for justice. The 1964 act also allowed federal funds to be withheld from school districts that violated integration orders. With these measures in place, the era of Jim Crow was slowly ending.

On August 28, 1963, almost a quarter of a million people demonstrated in Washington, D.C., to encourage the passage of a bill outlawing segregation in all public facilities.

Matters of Law

But there was another civil rights issue of concern to African Americans. Many blacks who tried to register to vote in the South were discriminated against. They were forced to take literacy tests that called for answers to one hundred questions about the U.S. government. In many cases, black applicants failed these tests because they had not finished school and could not read. White voters were not required to take a test, even if they, too, had not finished school.

The city of Selma, Alabama, had come under attack in 1964 by the U.S. Justice Department for unfair voter registration practices. Specifically, in order to vote, black Selma residents had to pass a literacy test administered by white officials. Moreover, it was not uncommon for teachers and other educated black citizens to be told they had failed. These practices were seen as purposeful obstruction of the civil rights of blacks.

As a result, one hundred of Selma's black teachers marched to the courthouse in January 1965. The teachers and over eight hundred schoolchildren who marched to show their support were arrested. Protests like this continued for three months. Violence directed against protesters was severe: Several people were killed, and hundreds more were injured. Dr. King organized a march from Selma to the Alabama capital of Montgomery in the hopes that civil rights activists would gain support for a voting rights law. On March 21, 1965, a fifty-four-mile march began, drawing twenty-five thousand supporters. As the march attracted media attention, Congress began to debate the Voting Rights Act. In the words of Representative Emanuel Celler of New York, Congress had no choice:

> Recent events in Alabama, involving murder, savage brutality, and violence by local police, state troopers, and posses, have so aroused the nation as to make action by this Congress necessary and speedy. . . . The climate of public opinion throughout this nation has so changed because of the Alabama outrages, as to make assured the passage of this solid bill—a bill that would have been inconceivable a year ago.[12]

On August 6, 1965, the Voting Rights Act was passed. It included measures that outlawed literacy tests as a condition of registering to vote and allowed federal employees to register voters whenever protection of applicants was needed. African Americans could no longer be discriminated against when registering to vote.

The civil rights and voting rights acts addressed some of the most fundamental rights of American citizens: the right to a public education and the right to vote. Author Williams comments on the significance of the civil rights victories of the decade: "Securing legislation was a crucial step in making the country more democratic. Voting, access to public accommodations, and an equal education were no longer matters of local largess [charity]; they were matters of law."[13]

Warnings of Other Problems

The years between 1954 and 1965 saw more social change and more court decisions and laws in the name of civil rights than any other decade in U.S. history. Yet, solving the problems of black America was a task that required far more than guarantees of these fundamental rights.

Malcolm X, who had done much to promote feelings of black pride in the African-American community, had pointed out some very basic problems with the civil rights movement. Despite changes in the way American blacks viewed themselves, which had given them a sense of pride and power in their ability to bring about positive changes in the areas of equal rights and voting rights, there remained very basic issues to tackle. Problems like discrimination in jobs and housing, often more difficult to define, persisted largely in the northern cities, where the worst civil rights abuses, such as literacy tests, had vanished well before the 1960s. It was these problems that, at least in part, led to an eruption of violence in cities in the North and in the West.

Martin Luther King Jr. led a march from Selma, Alabama, to Montgomery to protest the administration of literacy tests to blacks who registered to vote.

At the Breaking Point

The civil rights laws made it easier for middle-class blacks in northern and western cities to better their lives through good-paying jobs that helped them obtain decent housing. But for poor urban blacks, the laws had little effect. Often they were confined to poor neighborhoods, known as ghettos or inner cities, because of laws that allowed landlords and real estate agents to refuse to rent or sell to them in order to ensure that white neighborhoods remained segregated. Many urban blacks had difficulty finding decent jobs because they lacked skills and had received poor educations. For the poor people who lived in the ghettos, civil rights laws did not change the level of poverty that affected all aspects of their lives. Rustin spelled this out over twenty years ago: "Far from improving, the status of ghetto life seemed to be rapidly deteriorating, as housing, transportation, health care, and education systems moved inexorably [relentlessly] towards collapse."[14]

As a result, inner-city residents often had to cope with despair and anger. Some civil rights activists warned of the possibility of violence in the ghettos. In 1963 the executive director of the National Urban League, Whitney M. Young Jr., had written:

In teeming northern ghettoes, hundreds of thousands of Negro citizens—

It's No Mystery

The Voting Rights Act represented hope to the followers of the civil rights movement. But after the Watts riot, civil rights leaders began to believe that the law alone was not enough. Roy Wilkins, who headed the NAACP, explains this feeling in his essay "The Watts Rising," excerpted from A Documentary History of the Negro People in the United States, *edited by Herbert Aptheker.*

"There was no mystery to what was going on. In the civil rights movement, we had reached into the worst corners of oppression in the South; we had held the country to its principles and conscience and obtained the 1964 Civil Rights Act and the 1965 Voting Rights Act; but we had not even touched the misery and desperation of the urban ghettos outside the South. Nor had we come any nearer to correcting the economic sources of the race crisis. The day President Johnson signed the Voting Rights Act, it looked as if we were bringing to an end all the years of oppression. The truth was that we were just beginning a new ordeal."

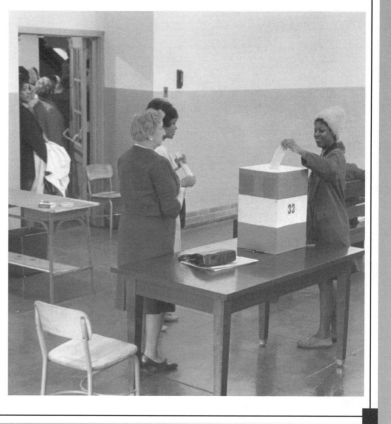

Elections became more accessible for African Americans with the Voting Rights Act of 1965, which outlawed discrimination against blacks registering to vote.

As civil rights laws failed to improve conditions in poor, inner-city, black neighborhoods, tension and violence in the ghettos mounted.

unemployed, ill-housed, disillusioned— are nearing the breaking point. Disorders have already begun. Violence could erupt at any moment unless swift and realistic action is taken to prevent violence by eliminating its basic cause.[15]

There had been warnings borne out by riots in northern cities in the summer of 1964. The first major riot since World War II was touched off by the shooting of a fifteen-year-old boy by an off-duty, white police officer in Harlem, New York. It began on July 18, 1964, just two weeks after the passage of the federal civil rights act, and lasted until the 23rd. One person died in the Harlem riot and 144 people were injured. Rioters also burned or damaged 541 stores in this large black community, which had been marked by antagonistic relations between police and residents.

A two-day riot broke out in Rochester, New York, the following week, on July 24, when a black person was injured by a police dog after the man attacked a white officer. Four people were killed, 350 people were injured, and 204 stores were damaged.

Throughout the month of August, two- and three-day riots took place in Chicago and in the New Jersey cities of Jersey City, Paterson, and Elizabeth. These riots were less violent than the July disturbances—there were no deaths, few injuries, and little property damage. In Philadelphia, however, 341 people were injured and 225 stores were damaged in an August riot; there were no deaths.

Each of these riots occurred after an incident between a black citizen and a white officer in an inner-city neighborhood touched off built-up anger and frustration among blacks. These are the conditions that were present on August 11, 1965, when Watts exploded. But to Americans who had followed the decade's peaceful civil rights movement, the events that took place in Watts were shocking. For the first time, the nation took notice of the extent to which acts of violent protest could coexist with a nonviolent movement—and most Americans were frightened.

Chapter

2 Port of Entry: Watts Before the Riot

In its earliest days, Watts served as a magnet for African Americans who came mainly from poor southern communities in Texas, Louisiana, and Mississippi. They had heard that Los Angeles was an attractive city near the ocean, with palm trees lining the streets and comfortable weather. They had heard that there were many jobs available in industry and in the construction of Southern Pacific railroad terminals in Los Angeles.

The Early Years of Watts

Word of the advantages of southern California spread during World Wars I and II. African Americans came from the South to fill war industry jobs in the shipyards and on assembly lines. The population of Watts soared. Los Angeles was a very segregated city. There were separate neighborhoods for blacks and whites, just as there were separate industries. So blacks coming to the city settled into Watts and formed a black community in South Central Los Angeles that was dubbed Mudtown by white people. Other sections of Watts were home to Mexican Americans and whites. Writing in 1966 of the beginnings of Watts as a black community, author Robert Kirsch said:

Watts was once a separate little agricultural community, populated by Negroes from the beginning, but remote from the rest of the city. It grew up against the bastions of the independent cities that line it on east and west, and filled up as its people were turned back from expanding into white residential neighborhoods.[16]

Mudtown became like a port of entry for black immigrants. Those who had good-paying jobs stayed until they earned enough money to move out and buy homes in other segregated parts of the area. But the majority of black Watts residents had no financial means to leave. With little option, African Americans settled into the Watts community. According to author Paul Bullock, many others who could not afford to leave "moved into deteriorating or substandard housing, absentee owned, and several hundred more moved to public housing projects."[17]

A Rapidly Growing Community

Conditions were disappointing for the rural newcomer. Many of the recently arrived African Americans had worked only on farms, so they were unqualified and untrained for the jobs they applied for in Watts. The jobs they did get required lesser skills and therefore paid less money than they had hoped for. Then, after World War II, more and more jobs were handled by machines, a change that took jobs away from unskilled workers. Many African Americans from the South entered the city handicapped by lack of education and experience; no training was available to them, however, and generally they were denied jobs. Since, in addition, Los Angeles was segregated, a black man was not likely to get a job in a white neighborhood. For the black man in particular, making a livelihood for his family became a difficult and often desperate proposition.

These problems increased as the African-American population grew. Within the space of twenty years, from 1940 to 1960, there was an eightfold increase in the black population of Watts. About seventeen hundred African Americans emigrated from the southern states to southern California every month. As whites and Latinos moved out of Watts to better neighborhoods, blacks moved into homes throughout Watts, not just in Mudtown. The community was not prepared for this rapid growth, and the federal government built public housing to accommodate the new population. Three projects went up during World War II and a fourth was finished in 1955. These large, two-story apartment buildings were overcrowded,

Children play in Watts. Black people who moved to Watts from the South usually did not have the skills necessary for well-paying jobs, perpetuating a cycle of poverty in the neighborhood.

and not all of them were well maintained. In the 1950s, more than a third of the total population of Watts lived in public housing. Far more people lived in these projects than planners had anticipated. It was not uncommon for families with several children to be crammed into relatively small quarters. By 1960, 60 percent of the population was under the age of twenty-five, indicating that the majority of Watts residents were young: youthful parents with young children.

The Los Angeles freeway system, completed after World War II, bisected South Central Los Angeles. The area east of the freeway, which included Watts, was mostly poor, while the area west of the freeway was mostly middle class. This newly imposed cutoff isolated the poorer neighborhoods from the rest of the black community.

The Ghetto of Watts

Watts had become a black inner city or ghetto. However, outsiders thought that Watts was different from other ghettos because unlike other inner cities, it did not have rat-infested, high-rise tenement apartments. In fact, after the 1965 riot in Watts, many Americans expressed shock that a riot could occur in an area that had looked a lot like white suburban neighborhoods. Author Bullock makes these postriot observations:

> Then, as now, as the observer moves from one neighborhood to another, he is invariably impressed by the diversity in the physical appearance in Watts. The neat, attractive, and well-maintained houses on Zamora or Pace Avenue south of 103rd—many of them

owned by residents who came to Los Angeles during the 1940's—would do credit to the most status-conscious suburb. Nearby are two of the imposing public housing projects, Hacienda Village, to the north, and Nickerson Gardens, to the south. The other two projects provide living space for about 5,000 persons in other sections of Watts. Elsewhere, shabby absentee-owned houses contrast sharply with better-maintained residences on the same block or around the corner.[18]

There were other contrasts within the Watts community. Some streets were unpaved while others were concrete roadways. Some homes were new while others seemed about to collapse. Nearly 87 percent of the area's homes were built before 1939, and about 20 percent of these older dwellings were in disrepair. In most cases, the homes were the property of absentee landlords, owners who collected rent on their buildings but did not maintain them. In some areas, there were vacant lots, while in others there were six homes built close together, leaving few places for children to play. Schools were far from the children's homes, requiring them to walk long distances to get to their classes.

Economic and Social Problems

While Watts may have looked somewhat different from its counterparts in northern cities, it did share their social and economic problems.

African Americans who tried to move out of the area were often the victims of discrimination by landlords who did not

A Blighted District

The Los Angeles City Planning Commission published a report on Watts in 1947 entitled "Conditions of Blight, Central Area of the City of Los Angeles." This excerpt from that report is taken from Watts: The Aftermath, An Inside View of the Ghetto by the People of Watts, *edited by Paul Bullock.*

"[Watts is] an obsolescent [outdated] area in which all the social and physical weaknesses of urban living are to be found. Some streets are unpaved, others have fine concrete roadways and ornaments; some structures seem about to fall apart, while next to them exist new, standard buildings. In some areas, a great number of twenty-five foot lots stand vacant, while in others six or more dwellings are crowded into a similar parcel. Recreational facilities in certain sections are few in number and limited in area. Schools are located in places where the maximum walking distance, rather than the minimum, is required of a great number of children. The shopping district on 103rd Street has little provision for off-street parking, and during busy hours the street is cluttered with double parked vehicles and is almost closed to traffic movement. Some of the worst interracial conflicts occurring in the past decade were in this area. The low rental pattern, the low assessed value of property, the high disease and delinquency rates, all reflect the blighted character of this district."

Watts was characterized by problems such as inadequate parking in shopping areas, low property value, and high disease and crime rates.

Black inner-city residents were discriminated against by white store owners who often overcharged them for inferior goods.

want to rent to black people. In 1963 the California legislature enacted a fair housing law known as Proposition 14, or the Rumford Act, which forbade discrimination in the sale or rental of a home. But this measure was overturned when the California Real Estate Association protested. On November 4, 1964, in a two-to-one vote, an amendment was passed that protected the "right" of all property owners to discriminate. The authors of this amendment reasoned that owners were entitled to safeguard the value of their property, which might decrease if African Americans were allowed to move in. This decision prompted Martin Luther King Jr. to say of California:

> It was the first major state in the country to take away gains Negroes had won at a time when progress was visible and substantial elsewhere, and especially in the South. California by this callous act

voted for ghettos. The atrociousness of some deeds may be concealed by legal ritual, but their destructiveness is felt with bitter force by its victims.[19]

Any African American who moved into a white neighborhood faced hostility and even the possibility of injury or property damage.

Watts residents were also restricted in their shopping. Most of the stores were located in the shopping district on 103rd Street. There were some black-owned businesses, like barbershops, but the majority of the food, clothing, and liquor stores were owned by white citizens who did not live in the area. Residents charged that while some of the white-owned stores sold quality products at reasonable prices, the majority overcharged the black residents and offered poor quality goods. Many residents were in debt to merchants who allowed them to buy on credit but charged high interest rates.

This arrangement made it difficult for Watts residents to pay off their store bills. While people could use public transportation and do their shopping elsewhere, fares were high and often it was necessary to change buses two or three times. As a result, few residents left the area, and resentment against local merchants grew.

An Impoverished Community

By 1965, the ghetto of Watts became characterized, as northeastern inner cities were, by poverty, inferior education, and crime. Nearly 56 percent of the residents of Watts were living in poverty, with incomes of less than $4,000 a year per family. About 29,500 people were unemployed. In 1965, nearly a quarter of the population received some kind of financial assistance.

Statistics showed that health conditions for residents of Watts were poor and medical care was insufficient. There were only 106 doctors for 252,000 people in areas extending beyond South Central Los Angeles. Of eight hospitals, only two met state health standards. Infant mortality for Watts was about 1.5 times greater than the citywide average. Many children were not immunized against smallpox and other highly contagious diseases.

Two Students Report on Watts

In 1964, two high school juniors, William Armstead and Richard Townsend, prepared a report of the conditions in Watts. They did not know of the reports by the city, yet their astute observations mirrored those of the adult analysts. This portion of their report is excerpted from Watts: The Aftermath, *edited by Paul Bullock.*

"The majority of people that do have jobs have the low-paying ones. These are the blue-collar workers in the semiskilled and unskilled professions and the white-collar workers, working mainly in the clerical field. For many of these workers who find it so hard to remain in one home for any length of time, repossession of property is common. They usually have large families to take care of and their income is generally barely enough to adequately support a small family. In a number of cases this results in discouragement, discontent, and misunderstandings within the family. The outcome of all this depression is cited as another major problem: broken homes. This problem of broken homes contributes to a number of community problems, a few of them being high mobility rate, high and fast rate of depreciation of property values, and lack or loss of self and community pride."

The miserable living conditions in Watts led to a high crime rate and an increase in conflicts between Watts residents and police prior to the riot.

Watts was also characterized by one-parent households of several children. An estimated 80 percent of parents of teenagers in Watts were divorced. These single-parent homes increased financial and emotional stresses for people already struggling to survive financially.

The education provided for children in Watts was inadequate. Schools were marked by overcrowded classrooms, poorly trained teachers, and facilities that did not even include libraries for students to use. The average fifth-grade student in Watts could not read. Two-thirds of students who entered the seventh grade dropped out before finishing high school. Furthermore, according to a 1960 Los Angeles census, about two-thirds of the adults

living in Watts had not graduated from high school, a handicap that hurt their ability to get jobs.

Crime was also a frequent problem. In the years 1961 to 1964, there had been several minor civil disturbances in the Watts area. In May 1961, a seventeen-year-old was arrested after he resisted an officer's attempts to remove him from a merry-go-round because he had not bought a ticket. A crowd of about two hundred African Americans blocked the officer from putting the youth into the patrol car, and he got away. A white person who tried to help the officer was attacked by the crowd. Seventy-five officers were rushed to the scene, where the crowd assaulted them with bats and bottles. Twenty-two persons

Troubled Youths

When researching his book Watts: The Aftermath, *Paul Bullock interviewed hundreds of Watts residents. Here Mrs. Williams, who moved to Watts in 1956, tells why she thinks there was trouble in her community with young rioters.*

"It's some of the people in Watts. If you got a good way they'll try to change your way to bad. There's a mighty few people what encourage you to do the things that are right. Everybody you meet, almost, is gonna tell you something wrong, and if you're weak you'll fall for it. So that's why I believe that most of these childrens that is in trouble, some grown people has swayed these childrens. I never believe that their mother would teach these childrens to stray, but it's somebody that they don't even know, it's somebody that is taken for a friend, that is talkin' against the mother and father with these children."

Two fires pour smoke into the air during the Watts riot. Most of the rioters were teenagers and young adults, and they were quick to join in the attacks, lootings, and burnings.

were arrested, fifteen of whom were under the age of eighteen.

On April 11 and April 25, 1964, there were more arrests of youths. The first incident occurred when six hundred people gathered around a young man who had been asked to leave a track meet, allegedly because he had been drinking. In the second case, a mob allegedly surrounded a disabled automobile and interfered with the ability of police officers to help the victims of a traffic accident. And on December 26, 1964, a group of jazz fans, mainly black, rioted in a Hollywood bar when a show was abruptly ended. The police were called and the crowd began throwing bottles at them.

Civil disturbance was not the only cause of encounters between Watts residents and the police. In one three-month period early in 1965, police reported more than a thousand crimes in Watts, including murder, robbery, and drug- and gambling-related offenses.

An Insider's View

Most of the crime in Watts, where the average age of residents was sixteen, was caused by gangs. Many teens who dropped out of school hung out on street corners with their friends. And their relationship with the police was a source of contention. In 1969 Bullock described these teenagers:

The older teen-agers search desperately for "kicks," a respite from the

---

Not a Real Ghetto

People outside Watts were amazed that such violence could occur in an area that did not resemble the ghettos in cities where minor rioting had taken place the summer before. In his introduction to Jerry Cohen and William S. Murphy's book Burn, Baby, Burn, *Robert Kirsch writes of this contrast.*

"Perhaps the most striking lesson of the many which are implicit in the fire and violence that have become known as the Watts riots of mid-August, 1965, is that a ghetto need not look like one. South Central Los Angeles, a long corridor of Negro communities, which was the setting for the worst race riot in the history of this country, is no warren of moldering tenements, no grid of asphalt unrelieved by trees, lawns, gardens. From the vantage point of airliners making their east-to-west approach to the Los Angeles International Airport, the observer sees no difference between the bungalow homes, the garish sherbet-colored apartment houses, the markets and shopping districts of Watts, Willowbrook and the cities of South Gate or Inglewood. For the freeway driver, intent as he is likely to be on the perils of high-speed traffic, occasional glances reveal antennaed roofs rolling by."

A police officer aims a shotgun at four people during the riot. A history of poor relations between the police and Watts residents was a contributing factor to the riot.

boredom and frustration of a ghetto in which there is nothing to do. Many of the youngsters carry their most prized possession—a "box" (radio)—from which "soul" sounds blare incessantly. Thousands of them will rarely see the world outside their ghetto, except perhaps in jail. The whites they know are policemen, probation officers, merchants, and teachers, and the relationship is often uneasy or hostile.[20]

The combination of a poor education and a crime record would prevent young Watts residents from getting jobs, causing a downward spiral that would keep them within the ghetto.

In the year before the riot, two sixteen-year-old students at Jordan High School in Watts, William Armstead and Richard Townsend, attributed problems in their community to the boredom among local youths. Their special report, "Watts: Its Problems and Possible Solutions," offered an insider's view of Watts prior to the riot. The teenagers said that one of the biggest issues in the community was that the young people had nothing to do. Athletic programs had been developed in the late

1950s, but Armstead and Townsend said there needed to be more than sports to occupy the restless youths. They wrote in their report: "It has often been stated that the number one motive for juvenile crime is not necessity, but sheer lack of anything else to do. Therefore it can safely be concluded that if there were more for the idle hands to do, there would be less juvenile crime, resulting in less upset in the life of ghetto individuals."[21]

Teenaged and young adult males made up the majority of the rioters during the six days in August 1965. As they faced the reality that little they could do would change their circumstances, some observers said, it was not surprising that they rioted on a hot evening in August. The McCone Commission, which was appointed by the governor of California to investigate the causes of the 1965 riot, reported on the general mood of Watts residents at the time of the riot:

> Thus, with the passage of time, altogether too often the rural Negro who has come to the city sinks into despair. And many of the younger generation, coming on in great numbers, inherit this feeling but seek release, not in apathy, but in ways which, if allowed to run unchecked, offer nothing but tragedy to America.[22]

By the summer of 1965, Watts was a ghetto facing serious economic and social conditions. The frustration of youth locked into a cycle of poverty may have been bred a generation before, but it reached a breaking point on a hot August evening.

3 The Arrests That Triggered the Riot

Tension between the mostly white Los Angeles Police Department (LAPD) and the mostly black Watts community was so high by 1965 that even a slight misstep by either group could have set off a confrontation.

The relationship between the LAPD and African-American youth, particularly males, had been a source of contention in the community for a long time. Youths complained that the police not only treated them rudely, cursed at them, and used excessive violence when arresting them, but watched African Americans more carefully than they watched whites. The young men felt that the police were quick to use standards such as how a youth was dressed and how late he was out on the street to identify lawbreakers. They also believed that blacks were arrested more frequently than whites, and that police often arrested blacks but not whites for identical activities.

But Watts was also a high-crime area. The 77th Street Police Division, in the heart of the riot zone, recorded almost seventeen thousand arrests in 1964 for theft, drugs, and prostitution. This was more than any of Los Angeles' fifteen other precincts. Many adult Watts residents felt that they needed more police protection than they were getting, and some complained that the police were not tough enough on some offenders.

Stop-and-Frisk Methods

The friction between police and the young residents of Watts revolved around a stop-and-frisk practice, whereby anyone could be searched if the police claimed to have probable cause to think that the person might have drugs. However, many in the community did not feel that officers really had probable cause to search the great numbers of black youths who were subjected to this procedure. Bullock wrote:

> "Probable cause," from a layman's standpoint, appears to be a flexible and subjective concept. Certainly, a youngster from Watts gets the impression that a policeman is empowered to detain and examine him for any reason that seems appropriate to "Irvine" [slang for white officer] at the moment. In many instances the cop will give no explanation at all, and, if pressed, he is often likely to say that the "dude" resembles the description of a suspect wanted for a crime. No one, least of all the youngster himself, can know for sure whether this explanation is honest.[23]

There were enough complaints about these practices to cause an investigation in

1962 by the Reverend James A. Pike, Episcopal bishop of California and head of the California civil rights advisory board. After two days of informal hearings, Bishop Pike concluded that there definitely was hostility between police and minority groups, citing as causes the low number of black police officers, the lack of human relations training for officers, and the feeling among African Americans that the police were unsympathetic to their complaints. The report criticized the police department for not trying hard enough to improve the poor relationship perceived by the community and for maintaining little contact with local minority group organizations that might have helped with this problem.

Though the Pike Report recommended consulting the U.S. Civil Rights Commission, the two Los Angeles officials who could have helped resolve the situation—Mayor Samuel Yorty and Police Chief William H. Parker—denied that there was anything wrong. In 1962 Yorty

asserted: "We have the best relationship with Negroes of any large city in America today."[24] Parker, in turn, said that Bishop Pike was totally ignorant of the Los Angeles situation.

Though the committee had little hard evidence about the validity of the residents' complaints, according to the Pike Report, the existence of numerous people in the Los Angeles area who believed, with or without justification, that these incidents occurred was in itself a serious problem. Said *Ebony* reporter Louie Robinson, "Many, if not most, claims are inaccurate, but enough of them are true to grate on the poor man's nerves, to harden the already bitter young juvenile, to incite—as it turned out—a riot."[25]

It was this conflict between police and an African-American male, twenty-one-year-old Marquette Frye, that set the Watts riot in motion. Though there are conflicting reports over some of the events leading to the riot, Marquette's arrest and the arrests

Watts had the highest crime rate in Los Angeles, but many young African Americans felt they were being harassed by police who stopped and searched them, using abusive language and excessive force.

James A. Pike's 1962 report found that the LAPD had few black officers, no human relations training, and was not attempting to improve its relationship with minority groups.

of three other people were seen by the African-American community as the fuel that set off the 1965 riot in Los Angeles.

The Frye Arrests

On August 11, Los Angeles had been sweltering under a heat wave for several days. Daytime highs had been in the upper nineties and the evenings were sticky, with temperatures in the high seventies. People were outside their homes, trying to cool off as best they could, making for numerous witnesses to the events of that evening.

Some experts say that bad tempers brought on by the heat made matters worse.

The traffic violation that began a generally agreed upon chain of events was considered routine. At 7 P.M. on Wednesday, August 11, 1965, Marquette Frye drove north on Avalon Boulevard, a main street just outside Watts. His brother Ronald, age twenty-two, was also in the car. Ronald had just returned from service in the army, and the two brothers had been out celebrating. Reports indicate that Marquette was driving too fast, about fifteen miles over the thirty-five-mile-per-hour speed limit, and that he was weaving in and out of traffic. Another motorist, a black man, notified the first police officer he saw. The officer, Lee Minikus of the California Highway Patrol (CHP), followed Marquette for six blocks. He caught up with him at 116th Street and Avalon, a neighborhood of two-story apartment buildings and numerous small single-family residences in the South Central part of Los Angeles, about seven blocks outside Watts. They were two blocks from the Frye home.

The officer asked to see Marquette's license, but he was told that the card had been lost the month before. Suspecting Marquette of driving while under the influence of alcohol, Minikus asked the young man a series of routine sobriety test questions, including his name and hair color. Accounts of some onlookers agree that Marquette entered into the test willingly. According to authors David O. Sears and John B. McConahay: "Frye was noted to answer all the questions, pointing out that not only was his hair black, but that he was 'black all over.' He showed the officer his ankles and arms to prove his point."[26]

Marquette later told a magazine interviewer that he had been trying to show off for the ten or twelve people who were watching from their stoops. The officer said, "You're quite the comedian, aren't you?" According to Marquette, Minikus didn't seem angry. Marquette told reporter Robinson:

> I had been drinking screwdrivers—vodka and orange juice—but I wasn't drunk because I don't drink that much. I told the officer I was only half a block from home and that there was no way I would have driven that far if I had had too much to drink. I even offered to walk the rest of the way home, because my father was coming home soon and he could come and get the car.[27]

Marquette failed the physical part of the sobriety test, and at 7:05 P.M. Minikus told him he was under arrest. As part of the arrest routine, Minikus radioed his partner, Bob Lewis, to help him take Frye to jail and to have his car towed. Lewis reached the scene on his motorcycle at the same time as another CHP officer, Larry Bennett, who was driving the tow truck. By this time, someone had called to Marquette's mother, Rena Frye, to tell her that one of her sons was being arrested. Some reports say that Ronald went home to get her. The small, forty-eight-year-old woman came down the street scolding Marquette for being drunk.

This is the point at which reports conflict. According to police accounts of the incident, Marquette, who had been cooperative until then, pushed his mother away and moved toward the crowd, cursing and shouting at the officers. He told the officers, "You're going to have to kill me to take me to jail."[28] Minikus and Lewis said

that at that moment, Marquette started swinging his arms and then tried to hit Minikus. Minikus said he had backed away and asked Marquette to come with him peacefully. Ronald and Rena Frye then moved closer to their relative. Ronald told his brother to calm down, but it was clear that this mild request would not work. The officers took out a pair of handcuffs and Minikus tried to put them on Marquette. Marquette ran off a few feet and then came back.

Growing Hostility

By then the growing crowd was getting hostile and the officers became worried about their safety. Lewis sent out a code 1199, which means "officer needs help." Minikus and Lewis got their riot batons from their cars and Bennett got an unloaded rifle and waved it at the crowd, an action which seemed to frighten most of the people. CHP reinforcements quickly arrived, and Minikus tried again to handcuff Marquette. The young man moved threateningly toward Minikus. Officer Wayne N. Wilson, coming to Minikus's aid, jabbed Marquette in the stomach with his baton. Marquette then attacked them. According to a report in *Burn, Baby, Burn*, "Minikus remembers that Marquette 'struck out at myself and also at Officer Wilson. As he tried to hit Officer Wilson, he also tried to grab Officer Wilson's baton and it appeared that Officer Wilson struck Marquette on the forehead.'"[29]

Reports agree that Wilson did hit Marquette. Wilson said that Marquette grabbed the baton, but Wilson got it back and hit Marquette on the forehead. A lump ap-

Nothing Goes Right for Marquette Frye

According to author Robert Conot, in Rivers of Blood, Years of Darkness: The Unforgettable Classic Account of the Watts Riot, *when Marquette Frye saw his mother arrive at the scene of his arrest, he became upset.*

"Observing his mother arrive on the scene, Marquette had moved around to one of the trees and toward the wall of the apartment house, some 15 feet from the curb. A couple of men were kidding him about going to jail. From his euphoric mood [high] he was plunging into despair. After two years of watching his step and not getting into any trouble, here he was in a mess again. Nothing ever seemed to go right for him. Nothing. . . .

'Let me have the keys to the car,' [Rena Frye] said to him. 'You know better than to drive after you've been drinking.'

'Momma, I'm not going to jail. I'm not drunk and I am not going to jail.' He pulled away from her.

The noise the people were making was increasing. As [officer] Lewis straightened up from the cycle he thought, for a moment, that Marquette had disappeared. Then he spotted him by the building and called to [officer] Minikus, 'We're going to have to get Frye out of that crowd!'

They started toward Marquette, whose unhappiness was increasing. As he spoke to his mother, his voice broke. He was almost crying. Spotting the officers, he started backing away, his feet shuffling, his arms waving.

'Come on, Marquette, you're coming with us.' Minikus reached toward him. Marquette slapped his hand away. 'I'm not going to no—jail!' he cried out. 'I haven't did anything to be taken to jail.'. . .

All the old anger, the old frustration, welled up within Marquette. What right had they to treat him like this?"

peared on Marquette's forehead and started to bleed. According to authors Cohen and Murphy, "The wound was not serious, doctors concluded later, but rather a stunning injury which left Marquette, according to Minikus, in a sufficiently 'weakened condition' to be overpowered."[30]

Minikus wrestled Marquette into the front seat of a patrol car and handcuffed him. As this was happening, Rena and

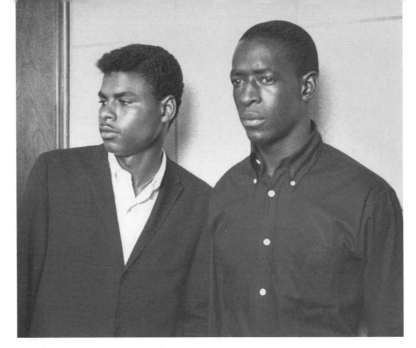

Ronald (left) and Marquette Frye, whose arrest on August 11, 1965, triggered the Watts riot.

Ronald joined in the struggle. Ronald tried to hit Lewis, who pushed him aside. Then Ronald grabbed Minikus. Meanwhile, Rena jumped on the officer's back and tore his shirt. Two officers grabbed her and arrested her; then they arrested Ronald after first poking him in the stomach with a baton. While these two arrests were occurring, Marquette was trying to climb out of the patrol car. Another officer, Harry Taylor, saw this attempt, shoved Marquette back inside, and slammed the car door. Encouraged by some in the crowd, Marquette tried to escape again, but this time when he was caught, his feet were handcuffed as well. After that, the patrol car drove away with all three Fryes inside it. It was 7:25 P.M.

Conflicting Stories

Though reports of the actual arrest conflict slightly as to who hit whom and when,

all concur that at some point, the police hit Marquette with enough force to make his forehead bleed and to cause him to double over from a blow to the stomach.

Marquette's recollection of the incident differs slightly from that of the officers. He recalls that everything was fine until the arrival of an officer who took his shotgun out of the patrol car; he explained to *Ebony:*

> The first officer who stopped us was more polite than most. However an officer talks to me, I always give him the respect of being an officer because there is no way you can win with a hoodlum attitude. Getting a ticket is nothing compared to all the heartbreaks you can have otherwise. If the officer in the patrol car hadn't come up [armed with a shotgun], I believe that everything would have been all right.[31]

According to the Fryes in their interview with *Ebony* reporter Robinson, nothing physical happened until the officers accosted Rena Frye and, as Ronald claimed, twisted her hands behind her back. Ronald said he asked the officer why he didn't leave his mother alone, since she hadn't done anything. He said the officers responded by twisting Ronald's arms behind his back and jabbing him in the stomach with the stick.

At that time, Marquette says he was pushed against a car and then hit with a club. "After they hit me with the stick," he said, "it stunned me and I just started swinging."[32]

Rena Frye was begging the police not to shoot her son. She said they were holding a shotgun to his head, and that after they handcuffed Marquette they had kicked and beat him while he sat in the front seat of the patrol car.

Marquette said, and eyewitnesses agreed, that he was kicked when he was shoved into the car. To many in the crowd

it appeared that not only had the officer kicked Marquette, he had also slammed the car door on his prisoner's feet. Virgie Nash was a spectator. "Why did you have to do that? That boy's already handcuffed and bleeding," she called out. "You didn't have to do that."[33]

At 7:31 P.M. the Fryes arrived at a nearby sheriff's station. Marquette Frye pleaded guilty to driving while drunk. His brother pleaded guilty to battery and interfering with an officer. Their mother pleaded not guilty to a charge of interfering with an officer. They were released on bail and for most of the duration of the riot stayed in their home. Authors Cohen and Murphy take up the narrative:

After the Fryes were released on bail following their arrests, the family rarely ventured out of the house during the days and nights of rioting that followed. But they closely watched the

Ronald, Rena, and Marquette Frye sit behind Police Chief William H. Parker as he discusses their arrests. The Fryes and the arresting officers told conflicting stories of the events leading up to the riot.

fiery developments on television. Marquette recalls thinking: "They blamed that on us—but what happened was on the surface for a long time."[34]

The Crowds Grow

By the officers' accounts, nearly a thousand very angry people had been watching the scene. Other accounts say the crowd was more like a hundred. When the patrol car carrying the Fryes left, so did many of the onlookers, although vehicle traffic in the area had come to a standstill. The people who remained agreed that the officers had beat and kicked Marquette. The owner of a nearby corner grocery store recalls the struggle:

> This officer had this man handcuffed in the car and the man was trying to fight. The officer took his club and kept jamming it into his stomach. When that happened, all the people standing around got mad. And I got mad. It's just too bad the officer couldn't have driven away and then struck the man. His action was breeding violence.[35]

Later the police reported that the arrest of the Fryes was handled quickly and efficiently. The sobriety test given to Frye was a standard California Highway Patrol test, and the use of a police car and tow truck was in accordance with Los Angeles Police Department procedures. After an investigation that included interviews with more than seventy officers and witnesses, the district attorney's office released a thirteen-hundred-page report that failed to turn up evidence of the use of excessive force by police on either Rena Frye or her sons.

But according to one eyewitness, "This [the riot] never would have happened if they hadn't kicked that man after handcuffing him."[36]

The Gaines Arrest

It was not only the arrests of the three Fryes, however, that set the riot in motion. A young woman was also arrested at the scene shortly after the Fryes departed. Joyce Ann Gaines, age twenty, had been having her hair done at Virgie Nash's beauty parlor. She and a friend, Virgie's daughter, Joan Nash, had been curious about the crowd outside, so even though she had a head full of pink curlers and was wearing a loose smock over her street clothes, Joyce went outside with Joan. The two women made their way through the crowd and asked what had happened. According to author Robert Conot in *Rivers of Blood, Years of Darkness*, people told Gaines, "The boy in the front seat, he was already bleeding and handcuffed, and one of the cops kicked him!"[37]

Gaines and Nash arrived as the car carrying the Fryes drove off. The crowd was dispersing, but there was anger in the voices of the people who remained. Conot reports that Nash told Gaines, "Come on, let's get back. I have customers waiting for me."[38]

Highway patrol officer James Vaughan was on his motorcycle preparing to leave. He had his back to the crowd, which was taunting the officers with jeers of "Look at the yellow-bellies run!"[39] He ignored them, but then he felt the moisture of spit on the back of his neck. Looking around, he saw a girl with pink curlers in her hair disappearing in the crowd.

He yelled at other CHP officers to get Gaines, and Sergeant V. G. Nicholson and his partner Gale Reed Gilbert plunged into the crowd. Though another officer advised these men to let the matter drop, others joined in and followed Gaines and Nash back toward the beauty parlor. The crowd, which was aware of what was happening, began to seethe with anger and would not move out of the officers' way. Another code 1199 was called, and cars that had been leaving the area turned back.

As Gaines made her way through the crowd, a hand grabbed her chin and pulled her backward. Reports say that she giggled at first, thinking that someone was playing a joke. Officer Gilbert dragged her by the neck and Gaines called for help. Nash grabbed her arm and yelled, "She hasn't did a thing, and look at what they're doing to her!"[40] Nash was threatened with another officer's baton and she let go of Gaines's arm.

The officers who were at the scene say they gently walked Gaines backward toward a patrol car; that is, she was walking on her own, not being dragged. Conot describes what the crowd saw:

The crowd's rage increased as police arrested Joyce Ann Gaines, a bystander who Officer James Vaughan thought had spit at him.

As she struggled and kicked, the pink curlers in her hair loosened and were scattered about on the pavement. Bent backward, wearing the barber's smock, she took on a pregnant appearance. Away from the crowd, out as she was in the arena of the street, hundreds of people could see her.[41]

Someone in the crowd shouted, "Look at what they're doing to that pregnant girl!"[42] Gaines, handcuffed now, kicked the officers, protesting and cursing at them that she had not done anything to deserve being arrested. They shoved her into a police car. The fourth arrest of the evening had been made.

A Growing Rage

When Joyce Ann Gaines was led handcuffed into a patrol car, rage began to build in the crowds. In Rivers of Blood, Years of Darkness, *Robert Conot describes the scene.*

"Along the two-block long stretch of Avalon Blvd., decades of distrust, of resentment, of antipathy, of pride ground into the dust had found a focal point in the arrest of Joyce Ann Gaines. In the manner with which the police had handled the girl people saw, or thought they saw, the contempt of the white man for the Negro. They felt, collectively, his heel grinding in their faces. They were stricken once more by the sting of his power.

'————!' a woman called out. '————! They'd never treat a white woman like that!'

'What kind of men are you, anyways?' another challenged. 'What kind of men are you, anyways, to let them do that to our people?'

'It's a shame! It's a pitiful, crying shame!'

'Blue-eyed white devils! We is going to get you! . . .'

The police officers, though they had long worked in a culture of antagonism, had never seen hatred of such intensity. [LAPD] Sgt. Richard Rankin—a sergeant of two weeks' standing—of the 77th St. police station, was the senior city police officer on the scene. To him, it seemed, and rightly so, that the continued presence of the officers could only incite the crowd further; that it would only lead to one incident after another, each bigger than the one before. Over the loudspeaker mounted on his patrol car he ordered his men to reform and withdraw. Once more they began disengaging themselves from the crowd."

The recollections of Gaines, Nash, and other witnesses contrasted sharply with those of the police. Joyce said that after listening to the crowd tell her what had happened to the Fryes, she had decided to return to the shop. She said she was laughing and giggling. Suddenly an officer grabbed her, and then he was joined by three more officers. She said she was still smiling because she did not know what was going on, until they grabbed her and dragged her backward into the street. Joyce told authors Cohen and Murphy:

> "He never told me I was under arrest or anything. He was just manhandling me." Joyce insists she did not resist, but recalls her hair curlers shaking out of her hair and falling to the pavement, and then: "A number of people were pulling me. So—they had a tug-of-war going with me. [Gilbert] had me by the neck—he was practically choking me to death. And the other ones were grabbing at me too and they were grabbing me until I didn't know what was going on."[43]

Another witness said that when the CHP grabbed Joyce around the neck, the crowd became furious, cursing at the officers, threatening them, and barring the paths back to their cars. When Joyce was put into a patrol car, LAPD sergeant Richard Rankin and CHP motor sergeant Gary C. Bebee ordered the officers to retreat to give the crowd time to calm down.

Meanwhile, the sight of a young, seemingly pregnant woman being mistreated by the police had been too much for the crowd. A man named Gabe Oss threw an empty soda bottle at a police car as it drove away. It was 7:45 P.M. and the sun was setting on Los Angeles. Oss's shattered bottle was followed by a stream of rocks, bottles, and bricks. Author Conot continues:

> And it was as if in that shattering the thousand people lining the street found their own release. It was as if in one violent contortion the bonds of restraint were snapped. Rocks, bottles, pieces of wood and iron—whatever missiles came to hand—were projected against the sides and windows of the bus and automobiles that, halted for the past 20 minutes by the jammed street, unwittingly started through the gauntlet. The people had not been able to overcome the power of the police. But they could, and would, vent their fury on other white people.[44]

In those final moments of daylight, the Watts riot had begun.

Chapter

4 Burn, Baby, Burn!

Within minutes of Gaines's arrest on August 11, the police decided to withdraw from the area to let tempers cool and to give the crowd time to disperse. The officers began to retreat around 7:45 P.M. Authors Cohen and Murphy describe this withdrawal:

> Any object that could be lifted and thrown flew after them. But the officers resolutely continued northward. Their superiors believed, with considerable reason, that for the police to remain at the scene of the Frye and Gaines arrests would only aggravate the friction. They felt the crowd would simmer down after their departure and that its members would return to their homes.[45]

Wednesday Evening, August 11

But the intent of the planned retreat from 116th and Avalon backfired. Various accounts of the Frye and Gaines arrests spread through Watts like wildfire. Many of those on the sidelines exaggerated what they had seen or thought they had seen. The rumors of the young black man being kicked and beaten by a white officer and a

young pregnant woman being dragged by the neck were fuel to the anger of anyone who heard them. Within the first hour, the level of violent activities increased. In addition to hurling objects at cars and buses, rioters blocked their paths, forcibly removing drivers and passengers from the vehicles and beating them. Many victims lost teeth and suffered broken bones. Rioters overturned cars, setting some on fire. Cohen and Murphy said: "Avalon Boulevard for innocent motorists, Negroes as well as whites, became a nightmare alley of flying missiles—whiskey and beer bottles, hunks of asphalt and slabs of cement. Anyone or anything strange, particularly in vehicles, was the target."[46]

Most of the rioters were males in their teens and early twenties. Adults on the sidelines did nothing to stop them. In their book, *Burn, Baby, Burn,* authors Cohen and Murphy suggest that many adults were probably afraid to try. Others just hurried home. One who was dismayed was Mrs. M. J. Ellis, a religious worker who lived in Watts. In her words:

> I came home from church and there were these hundreds of teenagers in the street. It was pitiful. Glass was all over the street. Those teenagers threw rocks at everybody driving through the area. I

The violence that followed the arrests quickly escalated from throwing objects to blocking vehicles, beating the occupants, and overturning and torching the cars.

saw a rock crashing through a white man's car. My husband and I prayed all night. I was scared. My knees were wobbling. I'm praying that God protects those policemen. I am asking God to help the police fight their battle.[47]

Residents started calling the police to report the violence. When it was clear that the police withdrawal had not worked and that the crowd was growing, more than one hundred helmeted police poured into the area. They met at about 8:45 P.M. at 118th and Avalon, two blocks from the Frye-Gaines arrest site. The sergeant in command prepared to send two ten-man teams to keep potential victims from entering the area. Officers on motorcycles then tried to enter the crowd to make arrests, but people threw rocks and bottles at them, driving them back.

The officers were under strict orders not to use tear gas on the rioters, and not to discharge firearms unless they were attacked. Instead, they gave chase with billy clubs, which many rioters later said had been used on them harshly. Some of the officers were successful in capturing and arresting rioters. But these arrests only infuriated the crowd. Some African Americans accused the police of inciting the resentment. Said twenty-three-year-old Bobby Daniels, who was returning from a fishing trip: "We got out of the car and these 15 officers ran up to us. They jabbed us in the back with clubs and told us to get off the street. They pushed us down and jumped on us, laughing about it."[48]

But plans were of little use to the police, who were outnumbered fifteen to one. Eventually the officers abandoned their attempts to make arrests and the

The rioters were mainly young men and adolescent boys; as the media flocked to the scene, the prospect of an audience to hear their expression of outrage rallied the rioters.

crowd spread from Avalon to Imperial, two blocks northeast of the arrest site, encircling a police command station. By then, television and radio crews had arrived, and many of the rioters scrambled to get their attention, eager to be on TV. Shortly before midnight, police decided to retreat again, believing that their continued presence would encourage the crowd to further violence.

Once more, the officers hoped that if they left, rioters would leave, too. That did not happen. Instead, the crowd turned on

white reporters and television crews who had begun filing into the area. The newspeople quickly became the targets of the violence as they interviewed some of the dozen officers who remained. Many African Americans asked to be able to give their version of the night's events for television viewers, but according to authors Cohen and Murphy, the journalists denied their requests. As remaining police left the area unobtrusively in groups of two and three, the reporters suddenly found themselves without protection. Philip Fradkin, a reporter for the *Los Angeles Times*, recalls that night:

> For some reason, the police took after a group of troublemakers on one of the four corners. Then the whole scene seemed to disintegrate—with people running in all directions. . . . That was when the riot really began. Until then, the people had directed their venom specifically at the police. But just before midnight, the pattern of the next few days of senseless, brutal, non-discriminatory attacks emerged. The people began attacking, not just the white policemen, but anyone who was white. After that, I'm not really sure what happened. I got hit.[49]

Rocks and bottles were thrown at the reporters. They retreated, but not before many of them were injured, some severely.

Around 1 A.M., the crowds began to disperse. By 2 A.M., only stragglers roamed the area. By dawn, the riot appeared to be over. Deputy Police Chief Roger Murdock

---

A Sergeant's Mistake

When LAPD sergeant Richard Rankin ordered the Highway Patrol officers to leave the site of the Frye and Gaines arrests, he believed that their departure would ease the mounting anger. His judgment proved to be wrong, though his boss, Police Chief William H. Parker, stood by the decision. In Burn, Baby, Burn: The Los Angeles Race Riot, August, 1965, *Jerry Cohen and William S. Murphy write:*

"Considerable criticism fell upon police for not immediately mobilizing officers from other divisions to meet the threat, and on the Highway Patrol for departing the scene of the Frye–Gaines arrests in the face of mounting mob hostility. Los Angeles Police Chief William H. Parker, who considered the original outbreak part of a nationwide pattern of civil disobedience, answered the next day: 'You cannot second-guess this type of situation, and you must protect the rest of the citizens of this community of four hundred and fifty-seven square miles. You cannot take every officer and rush them to a hot spot.'

Parker, often critical in the past of civil rights zealots, went on to say: 'You cannot tell people to disobey the law [in the sense of passive acts of civil disobedience] and not expect them to have disrespect for the law. You cannot keep telling them that they are being abused and mistreated without expecting them to react.' Parker was inclined Thursday to minimize the fury of the night before. He said he believed the violence at an end, adding: 'The magnitude of this affair is not as great as some prepare to make it—you should watch the misreporting done on TV from New York.' "

Police retreated from the riot area, leaving reporters unprotected. The crowd began directing their anger at anyone who was white, and several reporters, as well as their cars, were attacked.

had called it a night for throwing rocks at policemen, which he believed would quickly blow over. His words would prove to be very wrong.

The statistics from the first night included nineteen policemen and sixteen civilians injured, thirty-four persons arrested, and fifty vehicles, including two fire trucks, damaged or burned by rioters. Though the numbers were disturbing, no one suspected at the time how small those numbers would be in comparison to the totals five days later.

Thursday, August 12

Thursday was a relatively quiet day, according to Paul Bullock, who drove through the area on his way to a business meeting. Broken glass and the charred remains of cars filled Avalon Boulevard and the side-walks along it, but all day Thursday most stores were open for business as usual.

However, many city officials, including Police Chief Parker, were wary. The riot had ended with suspicious suddenness, and it was feared that violence might flare up again that night. Mayor Samuel Yorty warned Los Angeles residents to avoid the riot area and asked them to encourage their children to stay home.

To deal with the possibility that the riot would begin again that night, the Los Angeles County Human Relations Commission called a meeting at 2 P.M. in Athens Park, eleven blocks from the riot scene. Black leaders, social workers, ministers, teachers, and other people in the community tried to persuade the 250 people who came to the meeting—mostly teenagers and gang leaders—to stop the violence. Even Rena Frye, who had been released from jail on bail, was there. She asked the crowd, "Help me and others calm this situation down so that we will not have a riot tonight."[50]

Instead of cooling tensions, the meeting served the opposite purpose. Teenagers took the opportunity to speak into the microphone against white officers. One sixteen-year-old boy told the audience that there would be another riot that night, indicating that no one could stop it. When the young people got tired of speaking, most of them left.

At the end of the meeting, John Buggs, the Los Angeles County commissioner for human relations, asked for volunteers to spread the rumor that the riot was off and that the word was to "cool it." Gang leaders suggested to Buggs that white officers be removed from the area and replaced with black, undercover police officers. At 7 P.M., Buggs and other African-American leaders in the area took this suggestion to Murdock. The deputy police chief rejected the plan, since the LAPD had a policy of spreading out black officers, rather than concentrating them in the black areas. Of the two hundred black officers in the department, only seven were assigned to the riot area.

The View of Bystanders

In Watts: The Aftermath, *editor Paul Bullock compiled interviews with many bystanders and participants in the riot. One of them, Mel, had this to say about the riot:*

"But at first I was really frightened, because I had heard about riots in other countries, but never a riot in America. Never had I realized what a riot really was. . . .

Little kids was all out on the streets. Peoples were shooting guns, and the sky was just black, like the world was going to come to an end. People was running out, and there was this one lady, she was hollering, 'Stop, you peoples don't know what you're doin',' and all this different stuff. It was in the afternoon, and people were coming from work, I guess. They was white people, Caucasian people coming from work, and they would have to take this route to get to Bellflower or South Gate, down Central and Avalon. And this was just horrible because colored peoples over there they just took advantage of them. They even detoured the buses through the projects, and why they do this, I do not know, because I was giving it up. They was just telling them, 'Come on, you can do anything you want'. . . and it was horrible; I just didn't think stuff like that would exist, and I heard of wars and all this."

Meanwhile, crowds were gathering again in the streets of Watts. Chief Parker opened an emergency control center at police headquarters. Officers were instructed to surround the area where trouble was occurring and to try to confine it. They were told once again to refrain from using firearms against rioters until ordered to do so. Police were as ready as they could be for the evening's events, but the pattern of Thursday evening's violence was not like that of the night before.

It turned out that while responsible leaders had been meeting during the afternoon to discuss ways of preventing further violence, youth gangs had been preparing to continue yesterday evening's activities. Flyers had been made up and circulated by unknown sources inviting other gangs to join in. Molotov cocktails, which are bottles filled with gasoline and then plugged with an oil-soaked rag wick, had been stockpiled.

That night, these crude firebombs were ignited and hurled into liquor stores, churches, overturned cars, and piles of debris. Rioters began the uniting cry of "Burn, baby, burn!" whenever they started a fire. The phrase had come from disc jockey Magnificent Montague, who had introduced it on the radio six months earlier as a term that meant "cool it" or "let yourself enjoy the music on the radio." Unintentionally, the disc jockey had given the rioters a catchphrase.

False Alarms

As rioters screamed, "Burn, baby, burn!" they continued to throw bottles and rocks at officers and overturn cars and set them on fire. But this night they had a new target. When firemen came to the neighborhood in response to alarms about the burning cars, they were stoned and shot at. In the days that followed, firemen had to leave the scene of many fires to avoid being hurt or killed by rioters. In addition,

Rioters exclaiming "Burn, baby, burn!" used Molotov cocktails to set cars, buildings, and debris ablaze.

Who Are the Targets?

In Rivers of Blood, Years of Darkness, *Robert Conot describes the scene on August 12, after the first full day of the riot, when the identity of the primary target of the rioters' rage was unclear.*

"The intersection glistened with debris. It was like a garden of glass and metal and rock tinted with oil slicks, seeded with abandoned hubcaps, a rear-view mirror, and other accessories. It was midnight—the change of shifts at the factories. Workers, driving to and fro, came into the intersection. A few were attacked. Others escaped unscathed. There was no real pattern, no determining factor—Negroes as well as whites were bombarded. Timothy O'Seyre, at the corner of 119th St. and Avalon, tried to flag down drivers to detour them around the area, but he didn't have much luck. There was a little light—the city had been noticeably parsimonious [selfish] in installing street lighting in Negro areas and whole neighborhoods remain as dark as the bayous of Louisiana—and no man, white or black, was going to stop for a Negro frantically waving at them in the middle of the night.

It was newsmen, however, who were the primary target. A plump photographer, camera in hand, two other cameras dangling from his neck and bouncing up and down as he ran, was pursued down the middle of the street by a pack of kids—they laughed at him and let him go.

'Run, Whitey!' they shouted."

the crowds blocked the passage of fire truck and ambulance drivers trying to reach the fires. There were many false alarms, which some reports say were meant to lure emergency workers to ambush sites. Pawnshops, hardware stores, and war surplus stores were looted for weapons. When fire trucks came to put out three car fires at Avalon and Imperial Highway, they were driven back by gunfire. When a grocery store at the same intersection was set ablaze, the firemen could not get through until fifty armed policemen had cleared the way.

That night, arson activities increased as rioters began to target additional stores, stealing the merchandise and then setting the buildings on fire. The youths destroyed businesses, usually white-owned, that they felt had treated them unfairly by selling them high-priced, poor quality goods. They also torched stores owned by people to whom they owed money, ensuring the destruction of records of their debts. Black shop owners posted signs reading "This is a Negro-owned business" or "Blood Brother," in the hope that rioters would spare their buildings.

The Rioters Get the Upper Hand

Many white people came to see what was happening during the night of violence, even though police had warned Angelenos to stay out of the area. Robert Richardson, a black reporter for the *Los Angeles Times*, spent hours in Watts that night. He was amazed that anyone with white skin got out alive. He said:

> Every time a car with whites in it entered the area, word spread like lightning down the street: "Here comes Whitey—get him!" The older people would stand in the background, egging on the teen-agers and the people in their early 20s. Then young men and women would rush in and pull white people from their cars and beat them and try to set fire to their cars.[51]

As the riot progressed, the rioters seemed to gain confidence. Richardson reported: "The rioters knew they had the upper hand. They seemed to sense that neither the police nor anyone else could stop them."[52]

Several people, including black ministers, tried to persuade the rioters that night to stop the violence. Failing to make progress, these compassionate individuals turned to helping rescue white onlookers. One person who visited the area to try to stop the violence was black comedian Dick Gregory, who had been an ardent leader in the southern civil rights campaign. Gregory had been performing nearby, and he asked the police if he could try to persuade the crowds to stop their rampage. Before he had a chance to say more than a few words, he was shot in the thigh and had to be taken to the hospital. As reported in *U.S. News & World Report*, Gregory later said of that night: "There wasn't a street light left. The ground was covered with broken glass and bottles. The only light was from burning buildings. The police had their cars across the street for a barricade, and were crouching behind them. It was a real no-man's land."[53]

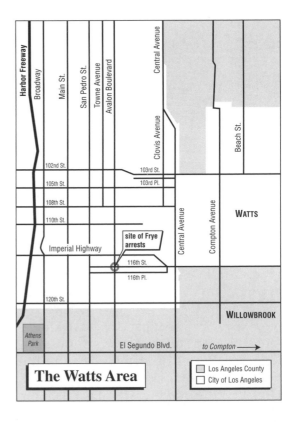

The Watts Area

Two buildings pour smoke into the air as they burn, overshadowing a torched car in the foreground.

The rioting continued well into the night, with rioters tearing up police barricades and cement-anchored bus benches. By midnight, about seven thousand rioters were swarming through the streets, smashing anything they could find in an area that spread to twenty square blocks of Watts and the surrounding region. Nine hundred city policemen, deputy sheriffs, and state highway patrolmen were on duty. As on Wednesday night, they were overrun. Though they had been given long-range tear gas guns, they were told again not to use them until ordered to, and the order never came.

By 3:30 A.M., Friday the thirteenth, at least seventy-five stores had been burned and many officers, bystanders, and rioters had been injured. New incidents of rioting were reported throughout Watts. The fire department had received twenty-five hundred calls. But, as on the night before, as dawn approached, rioters began to go home. By 4:00 A.M., the police department felt that the riot was at least for the moment under control.

At 5:09 A.M., just before sunrise, officers were withdrawn from the emergency control area. But, the worst was yet to come.

5 The Spread of Destruction

The fury of Watts's residents was evident in the increasing fervor of the violence. The rioters no longer confined their activities to evening hours. Now in broad daylight, they looted and burned stores. On Friday, at 8 A.M., angry rioters were surging through the streets of Watts yelling, "whitey," "blue-eyed devil," "Okies," and "crackers," all insults directed at whites in the area, shop owners and curious onlookers alike. The rioting spread to 150 square blocks, and the mobs grew so quickly that the police stopped trying to estimate their numbers. By 9 A.M. the shopping district along 103rd Street was so crowded it had become almost impassable. Molotov cocktails started seventy new fires. Police and news reporters were shot at. It was Friday the thirteenth, the day that historical accounts indicate was the worst of the riot.

The National Guard Is Called In

Despite the increased violence in Watts, city officials were hesitant to respond to the riot with any force other than police officers. Chief Parker ordered his men to work twelve-hour shifts and to arrest as many rioters as they could. During the two preceding nights, the officers had in effect only chased rioters from one site to another. Parker seemed worried that any other police response might seem like overreacting. He explained his concern:

> A problem came up which still is of some concern to me. We had some Negro officers in the crowd as undercover agents and one insisted that they were dealing with not more than 200 people in the area. This presented a dilemma. I couldn't justify calling out the Guard if only 200 people were involved.[54]

But when reports of burning and looting started coming into the precinct that morning, Mayor Yorty and Chief Parker agreed that the violence was out of control and that the police were unable to cope with it alone. At 9:15 A.M., Yorty and Parker decided to call on the National Guard, and the formal request was made at 10:50 A.M. Even after this extreme measure, Yorty was not convinced of the seriousness of the riot and left for a speaking engagement in San Francisco. In *Burn, Baby, Burn,* authors Cohen and Murphy report the mayor's statement: "By about 10:00 or so, I have to decide whether I am going to disappoint that audience in San Francisco and maybe make my city look rather ridiculous if the rioting doesn't start again, and the mayor has disappointed that crowd."[55]

Confusion in the Streets

Meanwhile, out in the streets, rioters increased their assault on shop owners. During the rioting the day before, owners who had posted "Black-owned" signs on their stores were passed over, with the vandals turning instead to white- and Asian-owned businesses. Stores whose white owners had treated blacks fairly also were spared. On Friday, the rioters were not so selective. They smashed hundreds of store windows, leaving merchandise exposed. Frightened storekeepers fled the area, abandoning

their stores, and widespread looting followed. About eighty small businesses were looted. By now, young men were not the only rioters. Women, children, and elderly people joined the crowds racing through abandoned stores grabbing all they could carry. As soon as a store was empty of goods, it was set on fire. A *Time* magazine article describes the scene:

> At 103rd Street and Compton Avenue, a mob methodically sacked a whole row of shops. The plunderers carted off radios, TV sets, clothing, lamps, air conditioners, rugs, musical instruments. A little boy of eight or nine sat sobbing his heart out on a pawn shop shelf. Every time he took a radio, he whimpered, somebody bigger snatched it away from him.[56]

Shattered glass and empty display racks in this store window attest to the extent of looting in Watts. Stores were broken into, stripped of all their merchandise, and set on fire.

Looters Took All They Could

In retaliation for what they claimed was injustice on the part of white store owners in the Watts district, rioters broke windows, stole goods, and set whole blocks of stores on fire. The following week, a Time *magazine article, "Trigger of Hate," described the gleeful attitude of the rioters.*

"A shirtless youth boasted: 'Man, I got clothes for days. I'm gonna be clean.' He added breathlessly: 'Tonight they're gonna git a furniture store on Manchester and Broadway, and you know I'm gonna be there.' 'Safeway's open!' someone shouted as the crowd ripped off huge sheets of plywood that had been hurriedly installed over the plate glass windows of a nearby supermarket. Looters swarmed into the store like ants, hauling out case after case until the shelves were bare. Then the huge, block-long structure was engulfed by flames.

The looters took anything they could move and destroyed anything that they couldn't. One booty-laden youth said defiantly: 'That don't look like stealing to me. That's just picking up what you need and going.'"

Looters race jubilantly from a store with three plundered lamps.

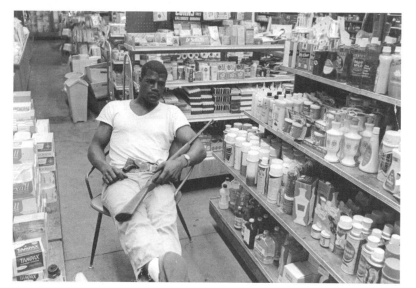

A drugstore owner, armed with a rifle and a revolver, defends his store from potential destruction during the riot.

One bystander noticed a mother of three small children in a looted shoe store, systematically trying shoes on them, as if she were a typical shopper on a typical day.

The pawnshops had been the first to be looted, since they contained guns, knives, swords, and bayonets. It was never clear exactly how many weapons were stolen, but the police estimated the number of firearms alone to be in the thousands, and the majority of these fell into the hands of snipers, people who shot at others—in this case, officers and white passersby—from concealed positions. But according to authors Cohen and Murphy, "Snipers, for the most part, proved sorry marksmen. Otherwise the death toll might have been far higher."[57]

As the day wore on, even some black-owned stores were not spared from the anger of the rioters. Store owners began to fight back. Cohen and Murphy quote one shop owner, armed with a shotgun, who faced down a mob by warning: "You may be my brother, but you're going to be my dead brother."[58]

Authors Cohen and Murphy say that many of the rioters had a gleeful attitude about the destruction. Reported African-American photographer Jimmy Thompson in *Time* magazine: "'They don't even know why they're doing it any more. They're taking stuff they don't even need.'" But one rallying cry never failed: "'We're paying Whitey back!'"[59]

Though police officers tried to stop the looting, it became clear that they would have to decide between saving lives and saving property. When they could, they wrote down the license plate numbers of cars of people who were rioting so they could arrest them later. In the words of Lieutenant Isom Dargan:

It got to this: the primary function of law enforcement is to protect lives and property—when you have to decide which to give up, property can be replaced. This function concerned us most at this moment. We knew any other action we might take might result in injury or loss of life. We didn't start making arrests [for looting] until late Saturday morning. It was more important to keep getting sufficient manpower in.[60]

Officers were also frustrated by a lack of orders. Confusion was prevalent. Protective helmets were in short supply, as were guns. Sears Roebuck, the department store, donated one hundred shotguns. Requests were made by Parker's office to precincts all over California for the loan of firearms. In the heart of the riot area, the lieutenant in charge, Lieutenant Mead, had no idea how many men had been sent to report to him and did not know what to do with them when they arrived. He had not been given enough information about what was happening in the streets. Because they lacked specific orders, officers continued to assume that they were not to fire unless attacked. Occasionally an officer would threaten to shoot in an effort to scare looters. Upon realizing they were not in serious danger of being shot, however, looters continued their activities, ignoring the officers.

Friday Afternoon

While the police were struggling to keep order, firemen were struggling to prevent fires from getting out of control. By Friday afternoon, the fire department announced that a thousand fires had been set. At one point so many fire alarms were ringing at once that the city's system short-circuited. At least two hundred stores had burned to the ground. Three blocks of 103rd Street were long tunnels of flames as stores burned on both sides of the

street. Black smoke rose in the sky, obscuring the sun. *Los Angeles Times* reporter David Reed watched from his office building several miles away, stunned by what he saw. He recalls: "I looked out a tenth-floor window at the newspaper and I could see the columns of smoke rising from buildings and all I could think of was the documentaries I had seen of bombed-out towns during World War II."[61]

The riot seemed to rage out of control. No sooner was one "hot spot" cleared than a half dozen others developed. By late afternoon, Parker acknowledged the severity of the riot, saying "We haven't the slightest idea when this can be brought under control."[62] Meanwhile, he waited for the confirmation that the National Guard would be sending in troops. As a result of a series of paperwork delays, this message did not come until 5 P.M.

By that time, the riot was located in four separate areas: Watts, which was on fire; a mile-long stretch of Avalon Boulevard, between Century and Imperial, which was also burning and where few officers remained; an area extending more than a half mile in either direction from South Park; and a ten-block stretch of Broadway, where rioters were just arriving to start new fires.

There were more than two hundred rioters for every one police officer. Along Broadway, officers were advancing on either side of the street, shooting into the air to warn off rioters. Rioters fired their guns. Bullets were flying everywhere. Twenty-year-old Leon Posey Jr. stepped out of a barbershop to see what was going on. He was hit in the back of the neck by a bullet that ricocheted off a building. No one knows who fired the shot, but Posey was the first to die in the riot. Around 9 P.M., a bullet fired by Deputy William B. Lauer hit Officer Ronald

An ominous sign reading "Turn left or get shot" warns people to stay away from the deadly riot area.

Ernest Ludlow; he died before an ambulance could arrive. Ten minutes later, officers fired at thirty-year-old Calvin Jones Jr., who had just looted a store. Two officers ordered him to drop the goods or they would shoot. According to an account appearing in *Rivers of Blood,* Jones dropped the goods but the officers fired anyway. Jones was the third person to die as a result of the riot. At 28th and Central, forty-five-year-old Homer Ellis had stopped his car in front of a liquor store that was being looted. He joined about twelve others who were carrying boxes of liquor from the store and put one in his car. Officer Gerald Ray and other officers, who arrived at 9:30 P.M., tried to stop the looters. Some officers were hit by liquor bottles. Ray and the other officers fired, and Homer Ellis became the fourth fatality. At 9:45 P.M., at Main and 82nd Streets, a crowd had gathered. Bullets were flying. Forty-five-year-old George Adams Jr., an African American, was killed. At 10:30 P.M., an eighteen-year-old looter, Charles Richard Shortbridge, was shot and killed by a shop owner. At the corner of 47th Street, tenants of an apartment building were warned that it was burning. One resident, forty-year-old Rita Rena Johnson, ran from the building and down a side street. That was the last time she was seen alive. Her burned body was found beneath rubble a week later.

Fires Out of Control

All day long firefighters had been working under unusually dangerous conditions. At a blaze that consumed Shoprite Food Market at 120th and Central Avenue, firemen tried to contain the flames. Lacking police protection, they were bombarded by stones and bottles thrown by the rioters. Some rioters whipped large sections of broken glass through the air like boomerangs. African-American motorists drove back and forth over fire hoses, blocking the water flow to the fire. Realizing the futility of trying to fight the fire, Captain J. Slade Delaney ordered the men to let the store burn. Just then two hundred

A City in Flames

In Burn, Baby, Burn, *Jerry Cohen and William S. Murphy describe just how extensive the fires were.*

"Pilots and passengers passing over the riot area in planes landing and taking off from Los Angeles International Airport to the west that Friday night saw what looked like great blocks of the city in flames. Next day, large portions of neighborhoods would be obscured from the air by towering plumes of smoke. *Herald-Examiner* reporter James P. Bennet, after flying over South Los Angeles in a helicopter, made this observation about the firefighters' experiences: 'It could easily be seen from the 'copters that firemen were being hampered in their attempts to quell blazes. As soon as engines would pull up, large groups of rioters would swoop in, throwing rocks at the firemen. In some instances, police would put up a cordon of protection around the firemen.'"

Firefighters attempt to get raging fires under control in the shopping district of Watts.

A convoy of trucks enters Watts as the National Guard arrives to relieve the police officers in the riot area.

tons of concrete and steel collapsed, trapping two firemen, Warren L. Tilson and Robert Laxague. "Then a strange thing happened," Delaney reported. "Those same Negroes who had been taunting us, throwing objects at us—those same people who had been threatening us, suddenly were horror-stricken. They came rushing across the street and began tearing with their hands at concrete and steel, trying to free the two men beneath it." [63] Laxague was pulled from the wreckage alive and with a few bruises. Tilson was the eighth person killed. A steel beam had crushed his chest and head.

And up the street, another mob set a new fire. Delaney said that at that point, firemen were no longer trying to put fires out. They were trying to stop the flames from spreading to people's homes.

The National Guard Arrives

Though 1,316 helmeted National Guardsmen had finally arrived in Los Angeles, at 10 P.M., it was not until around 11 P.M., more than twelve hours after Mayor Yorty and Chief Parker had requested assistance, that the federal troops were deployed to the streets. The new arrivals, sent out to replace police officers in Watts, which by then was almost a wasteland of burned-out buildings, appeared in jeeps with mounted machine guns and set up a command post at Jacob Riis High School. Infantrymen, advancing with bayonets fixed, ready to strike or fire, fanned out through the littered streets and assembled .50-caliber machine guns on tripods at intersections. Roadblocks were set up, and

Civilians Protect Themselves

One white person who bought a gun to protect himself was a resident of the Crenshaw district of Los Angeles' southwest side. Using the fictitious name of John Riley, he tells Jerry Cohen and William S. Murphy, authors of Burn, Baby, Burn, *why he made this decision.*

"Those people are burning up a section of this city. I don't care what their grievances are; it's no excuse for their defying law and order. So here I am, sitting around armed, expecting that some gang of terrorists will come any minute, invade my neighborhood and attack my home. Who knows how many other persons in this town are going to be waiting behind locked doors tonight with guns in their hands—like me, maybe jumping at the slightest sound, watching from the window for a strange car?

Did you ever think what happened to this city the last few years? Take this neighborhood. I've got Negroes living close by me here. And, hell, say I did pay only $17,000 for this house 20 years ago—it's worth $30,000 or more today.

Don't think Negroes were welcome here at first. The white people wanted to keep the value of their property. They didn't want Negroes for neighbors. . . .

But now it seems that they don't live so well in Watts and places like that, after all. I wouldn't know. That's the other end of town. And I don't think many whites got over there to find out how the Negroes do live. Watts always has been the 'other side of the tracks,' the place where the poorer-class Negroes lived. As soon as one got a decent job, he moved out. The more affluent ones come to neighborhoods like this and some of the homes they buy are pretty expensive."

Guardsmen were sent to the roofs of undamaged buildings to serve as lookouts for rioting.

Despite the presence of the National Guard, looting, shooting, and burning continued as calls were reported to precincts every two to three minutes. By dawn Saturday, ten people had died in the chaos. The latest additions to the total were a thirty-seven-year-old looter, Montague Whitmore, shot by an officer at 12:15 A.M., and a twenty-two-year-old looter, Thomas Ezra Owens, also shot by an officer. In addition, more than three hundred people had been injured. Friday night and Saturday morning marked the high tide of violence. Eighteen more people would die in the next four days, but the size and intensity of the Friday night conflict would not be equaled.

Saturday, August 14

In the early hours of Saturday, the first challenge for the Guardsmen came from a car that barreled down on a line of troops, hitting and seriously injuring one Guardsman. After this, Guardsmen were told that they could shoot if they thought they were in danger. Shortly thereafter, a forty-year-old motorist, Albert Flores Sr., was shot and killed by a Guardsman when he accelerated his car, seemingly intent on hitting the Guardsman. Other attacks on the National Guard troops brought a strong response, including the use of firearms to disperse crowds. After being fired on by a pistol and a rifle, one Guard unit opened fire for ten minutes, sending a group of rioters running. The Guardsmen swept the riot areas, first Watts, then South Park. By 12:30 A.M., these areas were considered under control. At 1:45 A.M., the body of seventeen-year-old Carlton Elliott was found by his mother. He had been shot in the chest. A thirteenth casualty was reported when twenty-three-year-old Theophile Albert O'Neal was found on a corner by firemen at 2:30 A.M. He had a bullet in his head. An investigation following the riot determined that his death was criminal homicide by an unknown assailant. Another man was shot by a Guardsman at 4 A.M. Forty-one-year-old Andrew Houston had been believed to be a sniper, although it was later discovered he had been unarmed.

By 4 A.M. there was a lull in the activities. But two more looters were shot and killed, bringing the death toll to sixteen. Twenty-eight-year-old Miller Chester Burroughs and thirty-one-year-old Leon Cauley were shot by police officers. At 5:15 A.M., when the sun was beginning to rise, another lone looter, Fentroy Morrison George, was shot as he ran from officers. By 7 A.M. looting and burning began again. At 9:45 A.M., a thirty-seven-year-old man, looting a liquor store with his twelve-year-old son and fifteen-year-old nephew, was caught by police. William Vernon King raised a gun at the officers, who shot and killed him. When King's body was taken away, people in the neighborhood burned the store.

A police officer kneels next to an injured man. Many people were wounded or killed from gunfire by rioters, store owners, police officers, and the National Guard.

By late Saturday, the riots had spread to 46.5 square miles, well beyond the original site. Ironically, it had been the day scheduled for the start of Watts's Second Annual Civic Improvement Week, an event organized by Richard Townsend and Bill Armstead, the two students who had written the perceptive report on their community. In 1964, they had managed to unite Watts behind the first series of civic improvement activities, which had included cleanup and a parade. Now their plans lay in ruins.

That morning, President Lyndon B. Johnson called the riot tragic and shocking and urged "every person in a position of leadership to make every effort to restore order in Los Angeles."[64] And he warned Watts residents that rights would not be won through violence. That day, thirty Watts residents attended a meeting at City Hall called by black city councilman Billy G. Mills. Three other councilmen also attended. The citizens urged Mills and his colleagues to find a way to communicate with the rioters, advising the officials that otherwise they could expect to see the riot continue. A major problem was finding responsible African-American leaders who could command the rioters' respect. But the state government also was faulted for not having recognized the problems of the blacks in the community before the eruption of violence. "If you had just been around enough, if you had gone into the area, you could understand what's happening. But it's impossible for you to understand it because you've never experienced it," the councilmen were told by Felix Bell, an African-American policeman whose dress store had been looted.[65] Bell had been unable to get to his store soon enough to put a sign in his window warning rioters away.

Governor Edmund G. Brown had issued a curfew, which as it happened was being issued at that time by the Los Angeles Police Department. The governor declared that the curfew was necessary because a state of emergency existed in Los Angeles County. Lieutenant Governor Glenn Anderson appeared on television early Saturday evening explaining that the curfew meant that any unauthorized person who appeared on the streets of the curfew area between 8 P.M. and dawn would be arrested. This strict rule is often used by the military during wartime, but it had never before been applied to a domestic situation in the United States. At the time, it was considered to be an extraordinary measure.

A Slight Easing of Violence

By midday Saturday, four thousand National Guardsmen were patrolling the area and seven hundred more were on their way from Fresno, about two hundred miles to the north. The troops set about "sweeping" three separate zones totaling forty blocks, the largest of which was a section of Watts bounded by Century Boulevard, Central Avenue, Compton Avenue, and 103rd and 104th Streets. The units formed battle lines that extended across a street from sidewalk to sidewalk. Guardsmen fixed bayonets to their M-1 and M-14 rifles and stalked down the street after rioters while police and deputy sheriffs followed them, arresting anyone who remained. The presence of the National Guard appeared at first to have little effect on the rioters. But gradually, as the Guardsmen surrounded them, the rioters began to disband and tried to regroup in other areas of the city.

Questions of Police Brutality

Though there had been no evidence of widespread police brutality during the riot, enough people believed its existence to make it a concern. Numerous reports like this one in "After the Bloodbath," in Newsweek *magazine, indicated the officers' lack of sympathy for Watts residents.*

"Even as the rioting receded, the anger bubbled on. 'These police, man, they got you T-rolled from the start,' said Ernie Smith, 25, chairman of the Afro-American Citizens Council. Outside the Best Buy Restaurant on Vermont Avenue, as the owner touched up a white-lettered sign on the window ('Negro-owned—Blood brother'), six Negro men talked of the violence. 'It's Parker and his police,' said dock worker Carl Williams, 27. 'Sure everybody down here's got a record. A Negro can't stay here a year without a record. They want Negroes to have records. Then we can't get those civil service jobs.' At the 77th Precinct, a disheveled Negro woman struggled away from her son and ran hysterically up to the sergeant's desk, shouting, 'Kill them! Kill them! I can't stand any more of this!' She meant kill *anybody* to stop the rioting. 'Very dramatic,' said the desk cop. 'Makes tears well up in my eyes.' "

A small group of rioters roamed as far west as La Brea Avenue, not far from Beverly Hills. In these white neighborhoods, residents were panicking. One sporting goods store owner reported that residents were lining up to buy weapons: guns, knives, bows and arrows, even slingshots. Reports reached police that there were to be raids on white neighborhoods and disruptions of scheduled events, including a charity professional football game between the Los Angeles Rams and the Dallas Cowboys and two circus performances. The events were cancelled, but the threats later proved to be groundless.

During the sweep of South Central Los Angeles, more deaths occurred. Twenty-four-year-old Curtis Lee Gaines was killed by an officer at 5 P.M. when the two exchanged gunfire. He was the first to die since the violent period between 5 and 10 A.M. An hour later, thirty-one-year-old Willie Curtis Hawkins was shot by police as he fled a clothing store he had been looting. A nineteen-year-old Mexican American, Ramon Luis Hermosillo, was shot at a roadblock set up by Guardsmen. He was the twenty-first to be killed. Twenty-two-year-old Joe Nelson Bridgett was shot by officers at 8:30 P.M. as he fired at them through the window of a store he was looting. Twenty-five-year-old Charles Patrick Smalley died next when he tried to drive around a roadblock. The twenty-fourth fatality occurred at 10:15 on Saturday night when officers shot a thirty-two-year-old

Troops guard a row of Watts residents. The rioting died down as the National Guard swept the area, enforced a curfew, and apprehended rioters.

Mexican American, Juan Puentes, who they thought had a gun. Twenty-nine-year-old Joseph Glenwood Wallace was shot by a Guardsman when he sped through a roadblock. Two nineteen-year-olds died Saturday night. In separate incidents, Frederick Maurice Hendricks and Eugene Shimatsu, a Japanese-American college student, each caught burglarizing a liquor store, were shot by police. Their deaths brought the toll to twenty-seven.

By midnight, thirteen thousand Guardsmen and police were patrolling the riot area. They had helped to arrest two thousand people. Meanwhile, the fires continued. For most of Saturday they had burned along Central Avenue. The Guardsmen and the police were not able to control this area until 3:30 P.M. At this time, Guardsmen rode on fire engines with their shotguns poised, an im-

age that was able to stop much of the sniping and rock throwing. That night, roadblocks were set up by the police and Guardsmen to catch anyone who might try to break the curfew. Finally, the massive show of force was starting to have an effect on the rioters. The curfew was also helping the Guardsmen control the riot. Authors Cohen and Murphy offer this summary:

Compared with the holocaust of Friday evening, the streets were relatively quiet. The only major exception was the burning of a block of stores on Broadway between 46th and 48th Streets. Snipers again prevented firemen from entering the area, and while the buildings burned, a gun battle ensued between law enforcement officers, the Guard, and the snipers.[66]

Two more people were shot before dawn. A forty-one-year-old woman, Lonnye Lee Cook, tried to drive through a roadblock. She died three days later. Fifty-three-year-old Paul Edgar Harbin was shot by officers when he tried to steal meat from a market. He died immediately.

Sunday, August 15

On Sunday morning, battle-scarred South Central Los Angeles was quiet. Some people ventured out to church while others sat on their porches and watched their children play.

Police now dealt with a new problem. Police headquarters received many prank calls. Rioters monitored police communications on transistor radios, and some tested the police to see how quickly officers would respond. The pranksters would telephone a report of a fire or shooting a certain distance from where such an incident was really happening, and then determine by listening to their radios how long it took for officers to get to the phony alarm. Their purpose was to try to keep law enforcement personnel out of areas where residents were actually rioting.

Four fire stations were set on fire that day, and motorists were warned to stay off the Harbor Freeway, which cut through Watts. Still, by Sunday afternoon, Chief Parker was cautiously anticipating an end to the riot. He reported: "We had lost control, but the power is now back in the hands of the police and the military. However, it doesn't mean that it is over."[67] By Sunday night, officials planned to have at least 10,000 troops on the scene. In addition, the Pentagon ordered into Los Angeles an 840-man U.S. Marine Reserve detachment, equipped with forty thousand rounds of ammunition. Until the marines arrived, about 13,500 Guardsmen and 1,000 police officers were working to control the violence.

While bands of rioters destroyed much of the community, residents struggled to meet their basic needs. Food was difficult

Although the riot was centered in Watts (pictured), rioting caught on in other cities in Southern California as well.

to find since almost all the food shops had been looted and burned. Drugstores had been an early target as well, so medicine was not available either. Many people did not own cars and the buses were not running, so most could not leave the area for necessities. African-American leaders asked for supplies, warning that if the residents went hungry, the violence was likely to continue. Governor Brown instructed the State Disaster Office to distribute food and other essentials. Several agencies sent provisions to the neighborhoods, though the need might not have been as great as believed. Authors Cohen and Murphy write: "As it turned out, the shortages proved overstated and the threat of a food rebellion never materialized."[68]

The Rioting Spreads

Throughout the six days of rioting, people sat before their televisions across the country watching the horror unfold in their living rooms. Many believe that these news broadcasts caused the violence to spread to other sections of California as people acted in copycat fashion. In San Diego, 102 miles away, there were three days of rioting and eighty-one people were arrested. On Friday night, there was rioting in Pasadena, twelve miles from the curfew zone. There, liquor and gun stores were looted and Molotov cocktails were thrown at police cars. The police were able to keep this disturbance under control. Pacoima, twenty miles to the north, had scattered looting, rioting, and burning. There was also burning in Monrovia, twenty-five miles east of Los Angeles. On Sunday night, after the curfew area in

Watts was quiet, there was an incident in Long Beach, twelve miles south. About two hundred Guardsmen and LAPD officers assisted Long Beach police when a twenty-three-year-old deputy sheriff, Richard Raymond Lefebre, was shot by another officer's gun as he was being attacked by rioters. His death was the thirtieth fatality of the Watts riot. Several fires were set Sunday night in the San Pedro–Wilmington area, twelve miles to the south. All these incidents were brought under control and never reached the severity experienced in Watts.

In Watts, there was one more fatality that night. At 9:30 P.M., in violation of curfew, Neita Love, a sixty-seven-year-old woman driving a car with her husband, got nervous when police tried to stop her at a barricade on Avalon Boulevard. When she accelerated her car, she was shot and killed. Her husband was injured.

The Los Angeles Area

The Final Days

Between 12:30 and 1:30 A.M. Monday, August 16, police received reports of shots having been fired near Broadway and 93rd Street. While National Guardsmen investigated, thirty-eight-year-old Aubrey Gene Griffen got out of bed to see where the shots were coming from. As he stood on his porch, he was spotted by the Guardsmen. He was the only civilian around. As he turned to go back in the house, Guardsmen shot and killed him.

At 4:25 A.M., a white milkman was making his rounds. To get his milk from the dairy, fifty-six-year-old Joseph Irving Maiman had to pass through part of the curfew zone. He was stopped by a Guardsman. He panicked and drove off, pursued by two National Guard jeeps. When they caught up with him, one of the Guardsmen shot him. He was the thirty-third person to die.

By the evening of Monday, August 16, the streets were relatively peaceful as few people opposed the strict curfew enforced by the police, sheriffs, and National Guard. The riot in Watts was declared over. Burning, looting, and sniping continued through Tuesday night, though as the days passed, the activity slowed. On Tuesday, August 17, Governor Brown declared the riot under control and ended curfew. On Wednesday, August 18, the National Guard began to pull out 10,500 troops. That night, the last fatality of the riot occurred when eighteen-year-old Carlos Cavitt Jr. tried to loot a burned store. Passing officers tried to arrest him, but he fled. An officer shot him in the head. He died two days later.

On August 22, eleven days after the Frye and Gaines arrests, the last National Guard unit left the area. Early the next morning, the emergency schedule of twelve-hour police shifts ended. Police activities returned to normal. The Watts riot was officially over, but in the charred remains lay images that the city of Los Angeles and the rest of the nation would not soon forget.

6 Charcoal Alley: The Immediate Aftermath

When the riot was finally under control, some people called the business center of Watts "Charcoal Alley" because the streets were covered with ashes from the fires. The streets were also littered with wrecked cars, broken glass, and hunks of concrete that had been dug up and thrown. These features, combined with thousands of brass cartridge casings from the bullets that had been fired, lined the sidewalks and made the neighborhood resemble a deserted battlefield. A *Newsweek* magazine article describes the remains of one fire:

> At Central and 103rd Place a Shoprite market lay in shambles, its frames charred and its shelves burned bare, the stench of its broiled wares permeating the neighborhood. Little flags— red, yellow, green, blue and white —still fluttered above the Huckleberry Finn burger stand at 106th and Avalon, but the inside was a formless jumble of shiny griddles and freezers.[69]

Coming to Terms

But visual evidence of destruction was not the only thing to emerge in the riot's aftermath. In the days following the riot, the city of Los Angeles struggled to come to terms with what had happened. Author Robert M. Fogelson describes the mood of the city after the riot:

> Overwhelming as are the grim statistics, the impact of the August rioting on the Los Angeles community has been even greater. The first weeks after the disorders brought a flood tide of charges and recriminations. Although this has now ebbed, the feeling of fear and tension persists, largely unabated, throughout the community. A certain slowness in the rebuilding of the fired structures has symbolized the difficulty in mending relationships in our community which were so severely fractured by the August nightmare.[70]

In addition, in the wake of the riot, the community had to deal with human loss, loss of essential businesses, and the problem of cleaning up.

The immediate feeling after the riot ended was that complete recovery for the stricken area would be a long time coming. On the surface, Watts returned to normal. Schools, parks, libraries, and public buildings reopened. Bulldozers cleared the way for rebuilding in some places. But in most cases, gutted buildings were left untouched. Police cars patrolled the streets with special precautions. Instead of one man to a car, they had two during the day and three at night.

The Toll on Watts

The human toll had been higher than in any of the riots of the summer of 1964. At least 1,032 rioters, officers, firemen, and Guardsmen were injured seriously enough to require treatment. Furthermore, thirty-four people had been killed over the course of four days. Twenty-six of those killed, three of whom were women, were African American. In addition, one Japanese-American man, three Mexican-American men, and four Caucasians, including two police officers and one fireman, had been killed. Investigations of thirty-two of the deaths were conducted through October 1965, a rather short period, under the circumstances. When the work was completed, twenty-six of the deaths were ruled justifiable, one accidental (Leon Posey Jr.), one homicidal (Theophile Albert O'Neal), and four criminal (Deputy Sheriff Richard Raymond Lefebre, fireman Warren Earl Tilson, Rita Rena Johnson, and George Adams Jr.). An investigation into the death of Eugene Shimatsu was canceled at his family's request. Only one person was actually tried for murder: Phil Brook for the death of officer Ernest Ronald Ludlow. The jury found Brook innocent when it was determined that Ludlow's death had been caused by negligence on the part of his partner, Officer William B. Lauer, who had actually fired the bullet that killed Ludlow. Author Robert Conot, who says

Despite the rows of destroyed businesses, a postman delivers mail on a charred, rubble-strewn street in Watts after the riot.

that the investigations were treated with indifference by both the white and the African-American communities, suggests that it might have been inaccurate to list some of the deaths as justifiable. The cases were never reopened, however.

Property loss was also counted after the smoke began to clear. Though most of the nearly one thousand buildings burned and destroyed had been commercial enterprises—food markets, pawnshops, and liquor stores—the county library at East El Segundo Boulevard was also burned to the ground: Twelve thousand books worth $95,000 were nothing but ashes. Some stores were able to reopen, but many people were wiped out financially because their businesses had not been covered by fire insurance. Their permanent departure cost the area an estimated 177,000 jobs. There were a thousand new claims for unemployment insurance benefits. Even before the riot, the Watts area had 22,000 people on welfare at a monthly cost of $900,000. Now that figure rose to a staggering $5.5 million.

Lack of Jail Space

The effects of the riot reached far beyond Watts. The city of Los Angeles was faced with the problem of what to do with the 3,952 rioters who had been arrested. Never before in American history had there been such an instance of mass arrests. Those apprehended were jammed into every available jail space in the city. Lincoln Heights Jail, which had been closed for many years, was reopened to handle some of the overflow. The food supply was inadequate, as were toilet and sleeping facilities.

The prisoners were processed in groups of ten, but keeping track of everyone was difficult. Many gave false names, so when people called to see if a relative was there, prison employees could find no matching record. Some rioters had been arrested more than once, which made it difficult to trace them. Sometimes there was no record of a person's arrest. As far as the sheriff's department was concerned, such prisoners did not exist at all. In the confusion, a woman who was seven months pregnant spent two weeks in jail, even though a judge had ordered her release.

Some of those arrested had been released on bail. In many cases, the bail money had been provided by bondsmen, who loaned the sum to the person arrested and then charged high interest on the amount until it was paid back. For families that were already struggling financially, this was an extra burden. Other prisoners pleaded guilty to charges of arson,

An owner stands in the remains of his barbershop. Problems that existed before the riot like poverty and lack of business opportunities were compounded by the extensive property loss.

What Can Be Done About Watts?

In an essay entitled "Watts Burns with Rage," reprinted in A Documentary History of the Negro People in the United States, *edited by Herbert Aptheker, author James E. Jackson, asks, What can be done about Watts? Professor Frank Hartung, sociologist of Southern Illinois University, provides one answer.*

"It will be as difficult—if not more difficult—to eliminate this sort of violence as it is to eliminate poverty. . . . Major social reformation, going far beyond the passage of civil rights laws, will be required to eliminate the threats of future upheavals in the Negro slums. Herbert C. Ward, Machinists' District 727 business agent and chairman of the Communist Labor Committee, spoke for Negro labor leaders in the Los Angeles area in demanding immediate removal of the Los Angeles police chief William H. Parker as the most universally hated symbol of the continuous and wanton police brutality and terror to which the Negro people are subjected. Furthermore, he called for: the immediate starting of slum clearance and new housing projects with public and private resources; the construction of a fully equipped hospital; the cooperation of all levels of government in an intensive program of placing unemployed and underemployed Negro young people in jobs or training for jobs at standard rates of pay."

burglary, assault, or minor offenses. Sixty percent of those arrested were convicted. Their sentences ranged from ninety days to two and a half years in jail. Rena Frye was fined $250 and given probation. The charges against Joyce Ann Gaines were dropped. In dismissing the case against Gaines, testimony was considered from District Attorney Younger who said, "I don't think they got the woman who did the spitting."[71]

The weapons of all descriptions stolen from pawnshops constituted another serious problem for the city. Only two thousand were recovered, though police were certain that many more had been hidden

for future use, perhaps by gangs. The riots also increased the sales of firearms to Californians who were fearful for their lives. Between August 16 and 20, gun sales in the state totaled 10,738, compared with the year-round weekly average of 2,000.

An Ominous Message

But city officials were able to handle these aftershocks of the riot. What was perhaps more difficult was negotiating the strong feelings of everyone from local citizens to national figures. Across the country, the

The self-destruction of the Watts riot produced opposing responses from Americans: Some empathized with Watts residents while others believed the behavior was to be expected from black people.

riot and its aftermath had touched off discussion. Some sympathized with and professed understanding of the rioters. Said Richard Gold, who owned a chain of furniture stores and had lost one to burning: "I can't condemn [the rioters]. These people should not be shot down like dogs. White people who were as poor as they would burn and loot if they saw the chance. What's behind this is pentup anger over poverty and miserable housing."[72]

Others expressed absolute inability to see how any community could use violence against itself. Some who were aware of the conditions that had led to the anger and frustration could not condone the destructive reaction of the rioters. Well-known evangelist Billy Graham said he believed that the Watts explosion had

taught people elsewhere how to riot, and he and others recommended an increase in police personnel in all major cities to prevent other riots.

The country was polarized on the issue of the riot. Some editorials of the time indicated that racists said that they were not surprised that blacks would behave that way. Others said that it was a direct result of how African Americans had been treated. While many leaders, including President Johnson, were appalled by the violence, they seemed to respond with sympathy to African Americans and called for more social programs.

Dr. Ralph J. Bunche, undersecretary of the United Nations, went a bit further in a statement to the press in which he said that ghettos must be eliminated:

The ominous message of Watts is that city, state, and national authorities must quickly show the vision, the determination and the courage to take those bold—and costly—steps necessary to begin the dispersal of every black ghetto in this land.

Continued social neglect and police abuse of the most oppressed and exploited Negroes, shoved as they are into ignored corners of the cities— "black ghettos"—are the tinder for future explosions in every city in this country with substantial population.[73]

Ralph J. Bunche, undersecretary of the United Nations, stated that ghettos, as concentrated areas of poverty and oppression, were all potential riot sites and should be dispersed.

Some people, like Chief Parker, had accused civil rights leaders of stirring up black dissatisfaction so that a riot was inevitable. African-American leaders, however, were horrified by the violence. Yet even as they argued that fighting for one's rights as a citizen was hardly the same as starting a riot, they pointed out that the riot had called attention to the frustrations felt by many African Americans. They indicated that it was hopelessness for the future that made the people of Watts feel they had nothing to lose by acting out their anger. Said Martin Luther King Jr. at a Southern Christian Leadership Conference days after the riot had ended:

> There is nothing more dangerous than to build a society with a large segment of the people in that society who feel they don't have a stake in that society; they feel they have nothing to lose. People who have a stake in their society protect their society, but when they don't, they unconsciously want to destroy it.[74]

"When, Dammit, When?"

While discussions about the riots raged outside Watts, conversations inside the community were still tinged with anger. Dr. King arrived in Watts on August 18, the Wednesday after the curfew had been lifted. He hoped to calm people's anger and suggest nonviolent ways of solving the community's problems. He had been warned not to go to Watts by supporters who feared—rightly, as it turned out—that a message of nonviolence would be rejected. At the Westminster Neighborhood

President Johnson Walks a Tightrope

In "After the Blood-bath," which appeared in Newsweek *not long after the riot, President Lyndon B. Johnson is described as walking a tightrope between sympathy for the rioters and disapproval.*

"Early in the week, Lyndon Johnson issued a statement neatly balancing an attack on rioting ('There is no greater wrong') with a call to attack its causes ('We must not let anger drown understanding'). In a speech five days later, he drastically shifted his emphasis. This time he delivered a blistering attack on the rioters: 'Neither old wrongs nor new fears can ever justify arson or murder. . . . A rioter with a Molotov cocktail in his hand is not fighting for civil rights any more than a Klansmen with a sheet on his back and a mask on his face. They are both . . . lawbreakers.'

But he came back, in the end, to the real meaning of Los Angeles: 'In twenty fields or more we have passed—and we will pass—far-reaching programs . . . that are rich in hope and that will lead us to a better day.' His fist crashed down on the lectern.'And we shall overcome,' he cried, 'And I am enlisted for the duration.'"

Association community center, the civil rights leader was greeted with ridicule. "Sending King down here ain't nuthin', man," muttered one onlooker. "He ain't gonna do nuthin'. But goddammit they better do something down here, brother, or next time it won't be a riot. It'll be a war." [75]

King tried to begin speaking several times. According to a *Newsweek* article, he said, "You are all God's children. There will be a better tomorrow. . . ." "When, dammit, when?" [76] a spectator roared. Though he finally got the crowd under control, King canceled other stops in the riot zone for security reasons.

But anger was not the only emotion that moved through Watts after the riot.

Immediately following the August event, there was a sense among the participants that they had achieved something important. Author Robert Blauner said that during 1965, while researching "Whitewash Over Watts: The Failure of the McCone Commission Report," he had found widespread support within the ghetto for the violent outbreak, even by those who had refused to participate. His account includes the statement that "[i]n the countless interviews and feature stories that appeared in the press and on television, Watts Negroes were more likely to explain and justify the riots rather than to condemn them." [77]

One of the reasons for community support was simply the attention the riot generated. Because of Watts, journalists, politicians, and Americans everywhere were, in most cases, made aware of the conditions in U.S. inner cities for the first time. And with the pledge by President Johnson to find ways to help people who were living in poverty and the formation by the governor of California of a blue-ribbon commission to investigate all aspects of the unrest, Watts residents had hope that their lives would improve. According to a *Time* editorial, "Many blacks secretly or openly think 'violence is valuable' because 'now people care about Watts.'"[78]

Another reason the community stood behind the rioters is the feeling that the violence had been justified because of the conditions under which the people lived. One letter to the editor of the *Los Angeles Times*, identified the writer as one who viewed the Watts riot "not as a Negro riot, but as a revolution of men and women who are tired of too few jobs, too little food and no hope for the future."[79]

A Sense of Community

There were some immediate, yet subtle changes. The riot had generated a sense of community within Watts. During the riot, three youth gangs representing the neighborhoods of Watts, Willowbrook, and Compton, all sections of South Central Los Angeles in which rioting occurred, stopped fighting each other and became one group of rioters. After the riot, the gangs reportedly worked together to clean up the area instead of resuming their wars. Because whites had been the target during the riot, most clearly evidenced by the rioters' attacks on white-owned businesses in Watts, a racial identity also developed afterward. Watts became a strong black community in which residents began to work together to rebuild their neighborhood under the leadership of the Student Committee for the Improvement of Watts. The group's scheduled civic improvement week had been interrupted by the riot. Now the work got under way in earnest.

Despite their anger, for a time, the people of Watts felt that the riot gave them the chance to have their concerns revealed to a nation they claimed had ignored them for too long. During a television interview, a man in Watts said: "We are never going back to letting anybody run over us anymore. We ain't going to just stand and look while they beat us. We ain't going hungry and ragged when they got more'n they can eat and wear. Those fires lit something inside my soul too."[80] For the next two years, this feeling was to be expressed over and over again in other U.S. cities.

Chapter

7 Why Did It Happen?
A Search for Answers

One of the most immediate effects of the riot was the spread throughout society of a need to explain how the calamity could have happened. Indeed, what could have motivated an entire community to torch its own buildings and risk its members' lives in violence? No one questioned that the rioters had acted against the law. The question was, What—or who—caused the violence to erupt?

Debate over causes and responsibility began even before order was restored. Some blamed social conditions. Others said the riot was the work of aimless youths. Some even credited the August heat wave that had hung over the city. Officials also exchanged barbs. Police Chief Parker blamed the Highway Patrol for mishandling the initial arrests that set off the riot. Others criticized Mayor Yorty for leaving Los Angeles at the start of the disastrous week to deliver a speech in San Francisco, and then, when he returned, not visiting the riot area.

Most of the criticism eventually settled on two subjects: the city and the police. The city, under Mayor Yorty, was accused of overlooking the conditions in which the

Blame for the Watts riot was placed on the police, the mayor, the poor conditions in Watts, and even the heat.

In "There's No Easy Place to Pin the Blame," published in Life *magazine soon after the riot, reporter Don Moser wrote of Chief Parker's attitude toward blacks.*

"The 77th Street Police Division, in the heart of the riot zone, recorded almost 17,000 major offenses last year, more than any of the city's 15 other precincts. It is an area of murder, robbery, theft and prostitution and drug addiction, and amidst such rampant lawlessness one would expect the police to be less than patient.

If there is some justification on the side of Chief Parker, he will not admit there was *any* justification on the other side. And when the riot did get reasonably under control, he stuck his foot in his mouth again by saying, 'We're at the top and they are at the bottom.' That, in a nutshell, is the heart of the Negro's complaint: they claim it has been ever thus."

poor, disadvantaged black population lived. Federal funding allotted to the city to alleviate local poverty conditions had not been fully distributed. The police department, under Chief Parker, was accused of brutality, harassment, and bias against inner-city residents.

Yorty Fields Criticism

Samuel Yorty had been in office four years at the time of the riot. He was respected by the state government for his management of an efficient administration, and he had reduced discrimination in the city's hiring. Earlier, however, when outside agencies had investigated conditions of black residents of Los Angeles and made recommendations for improvement, Yorty had responded cautiously. According to a *Time* magazine report, when the U.S. Commission on Civil Rights sent a team to the city to investigate black leaders' charges of police brutality against black citizens in 1962, "Yorty was downright hostile, [and] warned it not to serve as a 'sounding board for dissident elements and irresponsible charges.'"[81]

A federal antipoverty program administered by the Office of Economic Opportunity (OEO) had also met with resistance from Yorty. For a city to get federal funding to help its poor, its antipoverty board had to include representatives of private welfare agencies and also people who were poor. Other major cities had accepted this requirement of naming nongovernment board members. Yorty resisted, arguing that private citizens should have no involvement in determining how public money is spent. As a result of Yorty's opposition, only $17 million of a total of $37 million was released by the federal authorities for antipoverty programs that included the creation of much-needed jobs for young people. Another $20 million was held up while OEO head Sargent Shriver waited for Yorty to change his mind. The situation was explained in *Newsweek* magazine:

> Snarled in red tape over proper representation of the poor, LA's poverty war had been granted only a fraction of its budgeted millions by Washington. But even the available money hasn't been spent. Nearly $1 million of a $2.7 million grant to the Youth Opportunity Board remains unused; 3,000 of nearly 16,000 Neighborhood Youth Corps spots are unfilled; only 1,843 of 5,000 participants in the Work Experience program have been recruited so far. A recreational program for vacationing students did not start until days before the riot, months too late.[82]

In the wake of the riot, accusations flew from Yorty to the government and back again. Yorty, who felt that the federal antipoverty money might have averted the riot, blamed Shriver for the holdup in funding, while Shriver blamed Yorty for the confusion.

Parker Handles Accusations

Meanwhile, Police Chief Parker was also fielding criticism that he had ignored charges of police brutality from Watts citizens, and that anger over this treatment had led to the riot. A *Life* magazine article published shortly after the riot summarizes the differing views:

Inevitably, before the smoke had cleared and while sniper fire still crackled, there was a hunt for a scapegoat. The handiest scapegoat was the unbending, acerbic [sharp-tempered] 63-year-old chief of the Los Angeles police department, William H. Parker. Negroes who had taken part in the riot oozed self-justification and heaped blame on Parker and his cops. Others who deplored the violence saw it as the logical consequence of police harassment that they claimed had been the lot of Los Angeles Negroes for years.[83]

Parker had been police chief for fifteen years at the time of the riot. He was credited with having made the LAPD one of the nation's most efficient police departments. In fact, Los Angeles was known as "the safe city." Yet the department, which serviced an area having one of the highest crime rates in the country, was understaffed, with only ten officers per square mile, covering a total of 458.2 square miles. Despite the lack of manpower, the department had a very high arrest record—196,683 in 1964. Parker's officers were well educated and well paid, and none had been shown to be guilty of improper behavior.

Whether complaints of police brutality were a cause of the riot, and if so whether the causes justified the result, there had been evidence that trouble was brewing in 1962 when the civil rights commission met. No one had been able to find hard evidence of police brutality. And Parker had denied that any brutality occurred, adding that all claims of police brutality prior to the riot had been investigated by LAPD internal affairs and all had been determined to be false.

Watts residents claimed that they were victims of police brutality, while Chief Parker vehemently denied any discrimination against black people by his officers.

As Parker heard criticism of the role played by his officers in the rioting and before, the police chief continued to insist that his men did not treat black and white citizens differently. In a *Newsweek* article, he was quoted as saying:

> We have investigated these accusations at great expense to the taxpayer, and they are not justified. . . . [Police brutality is] just a word coined by somebody. . . . Remember, the police are the live representatives of the government . . . the ones that must maintain discipline and order. . . . I am disturbed at this popping away at the police . . . trying to blame the police while we have men down there . . . facing bullets. At least they could wait until we're out of battle. . . . But they all want to find easy answers to tough problems . . . so they pick on the police.[84]

While Parker was loyal to his officers, he also had a reputation of being outspoken. Comments about Watts residents like the following did not help his image. "The

riots started when one person threw a rock and then, like monkeys in a zoo, others started throwing rocks."[85] Though he was speaking only about the rioters, the remark was taken as an insult to all African-American people and gave his accusers further reason to believe the brutality charges.

No one disputed that Parker and his men were despised by many in the Watts community. Some Watts residents believed that the officers were racists who saw all black people as potential criminals. A *Newsweek* article that appeared in the aftermath of the riot reviewed the sources of this belief: "Negroes complained that police—many of them Southern bred—fail to distinguish between them, treating all blacks as 'niggers,' rousting them out of cars and frisking them on the flimsiest pretext."[86]

Regardless of the level of police brutality in Watts in the summer of 1965, there was ample evidence that perceptions of such behavior by black citizens fed the fires of the riot.

The McCone Commission

The ardent accusations on all sides forced the city administration to agree that the most serious charges needed to be examined. On August 24, Governor Brown appointed a commission to find the reasons for the six-day uprising, to determine whether it had been a planned event, and to develop recommendations to prevent a recurrence.

The nine-member commission was headed by sixty-three-year-old John McCone, a former director of the Central Intelligence Agency. Members included Warren M. Christopher, then a Los Angeles attorney, later U.S. secretary of state; Asa V. Call, an insurance executive who was one of the most influential businessmen in the city; Monsignor Charles S. Cassasa, president of Loyola University; Dr. Sherman M. Mellinkoff, dean of the UCLA Medical School; and Marlen E. Neumann, a former president of the Los Angeles chapter of the League of Women Voters. The commission's only African-American members were Earl S. Broady, a conservative Superior Court judge who had been a Los Angeles policeman for sixteen years, and the Reverend James Edward Jones, the most liberal of the group and the second black to serve on the Los Angeles school board of trustees. The ninth member, Thomas R. Sheridan, a former federal prosecutor, was the general counsel and executive director for the commission.

Given a deadline of one hundred days, the commission quickly hired twenty-nine staff members, sixteen clerks and secretaries, and twenty-six consultants. It heard seventy-nine witnesses, including Governor Brown and his advisers, local politicians, po-lice administrators, civil rights group members, teachers, and Watts residents, as well as other black spokespeople. The staff interviewed several hundred more people, including ninety arrested during the riot, and another ten thousand people were briefly questioned. The commission completed its investigation in three months.

The McCone Report

On December 6, 1965, the McCone Commission released an eighty-six-page report entitled "Violence in the City: An End or a Beginning?" The overall sense of the re-

John McCone headed a commission to investigate the Watts riot and offer recommendations to prevent future riots.

A Question of Improper Procedures

In the wake of accusations that the initial arrests were mishandled, an angry CHP commissioner Bradford M. Crittenden defended his officers. This excerpt is from his speech at a press conference, which appears in Burn, Baby, Burn *by Cohen and Murphy.*

" 'I have been deeply shocked and disturbed by Chief Parker's statements. During the period of the riot I was in and out of the chief's office. At no time did he indicate to me his presently expressed feelings.

'Particularly is it difficult for me to understand why, if my men are so poorly trained and qualified, as he now states, he continually asked for and received during the period of the riot the assistance of 60 or more Highway Patrolmen. If he has so little confidence in my men, why then did he knowingly risk their lives?'

In answer to charges that the CHP officers used improper procedures in facing the crowd, Crittenden said the officers acted properly, displaying shotguns when it became necessary, but keeping them unloaded."

port was that serious problems in Watts, including poverty and the animosity of residents toward the police, had contributed to the anger of Watts citizens at those they felt were responsible. The commission's findings were released with the warning that to prevent another riot, the issues identified would have to be addressed by the city. The report said, "The August riots may seem by comparison to be only a curtain-raiser for what could blow up one day in the future."[87]

The report indicated that only 2 percent of the city's black residents were involved in the riot. The commission also determined that the riot had not been planned in advance, although once it had begun, there appeared to have been an effort to keep it going. As evidence of the latter conclusion, the commission pointed to the distribution of handbills to incite crowds during the riot and the pattern in which stores were looted and burned. The report described the riot as a collective emotional outburst and suggested that the rioters had been caught up in the excitement of the moment. According to these findings, the six-day event in Watts was not a planned revolt, but an outburst that had no purpose: "It was not a race riot in the usual sense. What happened was an explosion—a formless, quite senseless, all but hopeless violent protest."[88]

The commission's analysis of the riot showed the absence of a single cause. The instigating factors came down to three areas: education, unemployment, and police relations. The McCone Commission saw no immediate cure for the problems of the Watts residents, indicating instead that the problems were deep and the remedies sure to be costly and time-consuming.

A Community's Problems

The McCone Commission reported the existence of a gap between the educational levels of whites and blacks in Los Angeles schools. They laid the blame on overcrowded classrooms in Watts and poorly skilled teachers. It was urged that classes in schools where blacks made up the vast majority of students be reduced by one-third so that students would get more one-on-one time with their teachers. It was also advised that the city create a permanent preschool program for all children from age three, to provide an opportunity to learn early language skills. In addition, "Violence in the City" recommended emergency literacy programs for schools in which children fell well below the city average, to be continued for a minimum of six years for elementary schools and three years for the junior high schools at a cost of $250 per student per year.

Recognizing that unemployment was the most serious problem facing the African-American community, the commission asked for job training and placement centers in all black neighborhoods. It also asked for state legislation to ensure the production of reports of how many black citizens the new programs had placed in jobs. The report's authors also suggested that legislation be enacted requiring employers with more than 250 employees, as well as all labor unions, to report annually to the State Fair Employment Practices Commission the racial composition of their workforce and membership.

On the issue of police brutality, the commission's report rejected widespread charges and saw no need for a civilian review board. Nevertheless, it warned that persistent criticism would undermine the effectiveness of law enforcement, and it advised that all citizen complaints be investigated by an independent inspector general. "Violence in the City" stressed: "Such programs are a basic responsibility of the police department. They serve to prevent crime, and, in the opinion of this commission, crime prevention is a responsibility

The McCone Commission cited inadequate education, high unemployment rates, and poor police relations as the underlying problems that caused the riot in Watts.

Criticism of the McCone Commission Report

"White on Black: A Critique of the McCone Commission Report on the Los Angeles Riots" presents the criticisms of Robert M. Fogelson. Here is an excerpt that appears in Mass Violence in America: The Los Angeles Riots, *compiled by Fogelson.*

"Put bluntly, 'Violence in the City' claimed that the rioters were marginal people and the riots meaningless outbursts. The rioters were marginal people, according to the McCone Commission, because they were a small and unrepresentative fraction of the Negro population, namely, the unemployed, ill-educated, juvenile, delinquent, and uprooted. What provoked them to riot were not conditions endemic to [characteristic of] Negro ghettos (police harassment and consumer exploitation), but rather problems peculiar to immigrant groups (resentment of police, insufficient skills, and inferior education) and irresponsible agitation by Negro leaders. Also, the riots were meaningless outbursts, according to the McCone Commission, not simply because there was no connection between the Negroes' grievances and their violence, but also because the rioting was unwarranted. Watts, for all its inadequacies, is not, like Harlem, a slum—its streets are wide and clean, and its houses are attached one- and two-story dwellings; nor are its residents, like Southern Negroes, subject to racial discrimination—to the contrary, they enjoy full and legal political equality. Thus, to prevent a repetition of rioting in South Central Los Angeles, 'Violence in the City' concluded, requires that police-civilian relations be improved, unemployment reduced, education upgraded, and civil rights protests suppressed."

John McCone (left) hands his report on Watts to California governor Edmund Brown.

of the police department, equal in importance to law enforcement."[89] In addition, the report highlighted the perception by Watts residents that they were being mistreated. A series of community relations programs to improve prospects for cooperation between residents and police officers was recommended. Suggestions included a human relations program to train the police on how to handle race relations, incorporating sensitivity training on issues of concern to the residents, and the reestablishment of youth programs such as the Deputy Auxiliary Police program, which had been stopped by Parker two years before, to increase positive contact between police and youth.

Among its final recommendations, the McCone Report urged the creation of a city human relations commission, which would, among other things, communicate with the public about how to eliminate prejudice

A Difficult Task

The McCone Commission's report, "Violence in the City: An End or a Beginning?" received much criticism for its lack of understanding of the life circumstances of inner-city blacks. However, the members of the commission were given a difficult task: to examine and report in only a hundred days on the worst riot the country had ever seen. This excerpt from the report is taken from Mass Violence in America, *compiled by Robert M. Fogelson.*

"The Governor charged the Commission to 'probe deeply the immediate and underlying causes of the riots.' Therefore, the search for causes, both immediate and long-term, has been our primary objective over the past 100 days. We have all recognized our obligation to find, if we can, the seed bed of violence. This search has taken us to the disciplines of psychology, sociology, economics, and political science, as well as to the curfew area itself. We have crossed and re-crossed various fields of knowledge relevant to our endeavor. In doing so, we have drawn on the expertise and experience of people at many levels of government, in California's leading universities, in business and labor organizations here and elsewhere, as well as of private individuals with long experience in the central Los Angeles area.

It would have simplified our task and assisted enormously in the formulation of our conclusions and recommendations if we could have identified a single cause for the disorder. This was not to be. It is our firm conclusion that no single circumstance can be identified as the sole reason for the August riots; the causes and contributing circumstances were many. It is these circumstances that the balance of the report probes."

and discrimination in employment, housing, education, and public facilities.

Reaction to the McCone Report

Immediately upon its release, the report received both positive and negative comments. Many of the programs outlined in the report were seen as innovative. The preschool program and the idea of reducing class sizes in poor areas, for example, paved the way for modern governmental programs. But civil rights activists criticized the choice of appointees to the commission, as well as its methods of obtaining information; it followed that the commission's findings, too, would come in for criticism.

There were questions about the choice of John McCone to head the group. Critics felt that the former CIA director's style and his attitudes toward African Americans influenced how the study was conducted and alienated many in the black community. Samuel L. Williams, a Los Angeles lawyer who was one of the few African Americans on the commission's staff, said, "Mr. McCone was the kind of guy who knew what caused it all before he started."[90] Williams indicated that McCone had predetermined what the report would say and perhaps did not weigh the evidence carefully. McCone had not had any prior contact with the community of Watts, so many critics believed he would not be able to make valid comments on conditions there. Critics argued that the members of the commission represented views of white, middle-class people who did not understand the conditions under

John McCone's commission was criticized for investigating the riot from a "white, middle-class" point of view that did not consider enough input from Watts residents.

which black people lived and therefore would be hindered in determining what had caused the riot.

Critics further contended that the commission had not held open hearings, with the result that only a small group of Watts residents had been allowed to speak about their complaints. McCone, who died in 1991, had defended the commission's decision not to hold open hearings for fear of turning the proceedings into a forum of exaggerations. Regardless of whether these concerns were justified, many, including commission member James Edward Jones, the clergyman, said that this move alienated the investigators from the very people their work would affect, the black community.

A *Los Angeles Times* article written twenty-seven years later sets out these charges against the McCone Commission:

Virtually all of its meetings were held behind closed doors under rigid security at a downtown office. The reports of knowledgeable social scientists frequently were ignored, and civil rights activists were portrayed more as precipitant [instigators] of the riots than as participants in a movement to overcome what they viewed as centuries of injustice.[91]

Many claim that the method of gathering information led to skewed findings that undermined the commission's announced goals and did not offer any new information about the conditions in Watts. Author Robert Blauner points out: "As Los Angeles councilman Bill Mills commented, most of the material in the report documents conditions in the Negro ghetto that have been common knowledge to sociologists and the informed public for a generation."[92]

Rev. Jones was so disheartened by the report that he refused to sign it. He was particularly upset by the commission's conclusion that civil rights leaders had incited the riot by making accusations of racial inequality in the years prior to the August 1965 events that then made the Watts residents angry enough to riot. The report said:

To be sure, the civil rights controversy has never been the issue in our community that it has been in the South. However, the accusations of the leaders of the national movement have been picked up by many local voices and have been echoed throughout the Negro community here.[93]

In response, Rev. Jones issued a statement, which was included in the McCone Report, objecting to the practice of stifling the complaints of ghetto dwellers:

I do not believe it is the function of this commission to put a lid on the protest registered by those sweltering in ghettos of the urban areas of our country. . . . Protest against forces which reduce individuals to second-class citizens, political, cultural and psychological nonentities, are part of the celebrated American tradition. As long as an individual "stands outside looking in" he is not part of that society: that society cannot say that he does not have a right to protest.[94]

A Misunderstanding?

The strongest criticisms leveled at the McCone Commission were failure to understand the frustrations that would drive a group of people to the level of violence displayed in Watts and ignoring residents' true complaints. Less than two months after the report was issued, Bayard Rustin, one of the organizers of the 1963 March on Washington and a longtime advocate of civil rights, was among those who challenged the report. Rustin denied that the riot had been senseless. Watts residents, he said, had very real complaints against conditions in their community and had rioted because they were tired of waiting for things to change for the better.

Regarding education, Rustin said the report had nothing to say about what could be done to educate adolescents who dropped out of school. Moreover, it failed

Civil rights leader Bayard Rustin disagreed with the McCone Commission's conclusion that the riot had been senseless, saying that the rioters' actions stemmed from legitimate complaints.

to recommend desegregation of the Watts schools, a measure he believed would have improved the education level of the black students. Instead, he said, the report seemed to condone the continuation of separate-but-equal schooling in Watts.

In terms of unemployment, Rustin observed that the commission's recommendation to create fifty thousand new jobs lacked suggestions for practical training.

Rather, it was proposed that Watts residents be trained to improve their attitudes about work, with a view to helping motivate them to keep jobs. Rustin commented, "The truth of the matter is that Negro youths cannot change their attitudes until they see that they can get jobs."[95]

Rustin also criticized the report's dismissal of allegations of police brutality against black residents, pointing out that the commission based its conclusion on Chief Parker's statements and failed to consider evidence submitted by the people within the community. Author Robert M. Fogelson, in his report for the President's Commission on Law Enforcement and Administration of Justice in 1966, said that the many Watts residents who had criminal records would be at a disadvantage in applying for these new jobs. Also, he said, the report did not mention the discrimination residents believed they experienced when job hunting.

Rustin, Fogelson, and others wrote that "Violence in the City: An End or a Beginning?" indicated that the McCone Commission had misunderstood the character and implications of the riot. They claimed that in proposing solutions to obvious issues like education, unemployment, and police response to black citizens, the McCone Commission ignored the segregation that lay beneath the problems of the people of Watts and of all inner-city African Americans. To civil rights leaders, these concerns over misunderstandings on the part of government agencies and officials gained in importance as the movement entered the second half of the decade.

8 The Legacy of Watts

During the cleanup of battered Watts and the implementation of some of the programs recommended by the McCone Commission, people experienced a renewed sense of hope for positive change. But others debated the question of whether this sense of promise might have been achieved without violence. Though most Americans sympathized with the residents of the South Central Los Angeles ghetto, they feared that if a riot could happen in Los Angeles, it could happen anywhere.

Turning Point in the Civil Rights Struggle

Perhaps the single greatest legacy of the Watts riot was to serve as a turning point in the civil rights struggle. While the nonviolent demonstrations of civil rights activists had brought black and white people together, the riot had pulled them apart. Many whites who had supported the movement worried that a new pattern of organized violence as a means of improving conditions in inner cities would be the next wave of the civil rights movement. This issue divided the black community as well. Advocates of nonviolence like Martin

Luther King Jr. spoke out repeatedly against the use of force to bring about change. He argued that the civil rights movement should focus on improving the economic and social conditions of inner-city blacks through continuing peaceful measures. In 1966 he strongly opposed the suggestion that the movement was using a strategy of violence:

> So far, only the police through their fears and prejudice have goaded our people to riot. And once the riot starts, only the police or the National Guard have been able to put an end to them. This demonstrates that these violent eruptions are unplanned, uncontrollable temper tantrums brought on by long-neglected poverty, humiliation, oppression, and exploitation. Violence as a strategy for social change in America is nonexistent. All the sound and fury seems but a posturing of cowards whose bold talk produces no action and signifies nothing.[96]

Meanwhile, though, militant groups gained in popularity with young African Americans. The strongest followers were ghetto residents who were frustrated with the philosophy of nonviolence. In Oakland, California, two college students, Huey P. Newton and Bobby Seale, formed the Black Panther Party for Self-Defense in October 1966. They monitored the actions of local police and carried guns to intimidate law enforcement personnel. The party's ten-point plan included an immediate end to police brutality and demands for full employment and decent housing for blacks. The organization encouraged the teaching of black history so that youths could develop a sense of racial identity and pride. By 1968 Black Panther groups had formed in twenty-five cities, including Los Angeles.

The slogan "black power" was popularized in 1966 by, among others, Stokely Carmichael, chairman of the Student Nonviolent Coordinating Committee. The initial philosophy of black power was to try to elect more African Americans to political office. However, as it grew in popularity,

Bobby Seale (left) and Huey P. Newton formed the Black Panther Party in 1966 to promote self-defense, employment, and decent housing for black people.

Rising Consciousness of Black People

The Black Panther Party, founded in October 1966 in northern California by Huey P. Newton and Bobby Seale, advocated black nationalism and self-defense. Its goals for blacks were self-determination, full employment, decent housing, an end to exploitation, exemption from military service, and an end to police brutality. They monitored the activities of the Oakland Police Department. The Black Panthers were viewed as local heroes, brazenly displaying guns to intimidate the police. In this excerpt from Revolutionary Suicide, *reprinted in* Eyes on the Prize, *the civil rights reader compiled by Juan Williams, Newton explains the philosophy of the organization.*

"We had seen Watts rise up the previous year. We had seen how the police attacked the Watts community after causing the trouble in the first place. We had seen Martin Luther King come to Watts in an effort to calm the people, and we had seen his philosophy of nonviolence rejected. Black people had been taught nonviolence; it was deep in us. What good, however, was nonviolence when the police were determined to rule by force? . . . We had seen all this, and we recognized that the rising consciousness of Black people was almost at the point of explosion."

Huey P. Newton, cofounder of the Black Panthers.

black power came to mean black sepa-
ratism, the idea that African Americans
should refuse to integrate into white society. The immediate impact of the concept
of black power was to increase fear of
blacks among white people. It also caused a
split with civil rights leaders who continued
to fight for integration.

Riots Develop in 150 Cities

Yet, in the next two years, it became clear
to Americans that regardless of whether
the violence in Watts had been premedi-
tated, African Americans in 150 other
cities were reacting to conditions in their
own communities in the same way. In 1967
a riot that surpassed Watts in loss of life
and damage to property occurred in Detroit, Michigan. About forty people died
and two thousand were wounded. About
$45 million dollars worth of property was
destroyed by fire. This riot, like most of
the others in the two years after Watts, was
touched off by a confrontation with white
police officers, and the pattern of the rioters was in each case to damage property
that they felt white people had acquired at
the expense of blacks.

In the wake of Detroit, King stressed
that the violence of the riots ultimately did
nothing to improve the lives of African
Americans. Instead it hurt them. He said:

> The futility of violence in the struggle
> for racial injustice has been tragically
> etched in all the recent Negro riots.
> Yesterday, I tried to analyze the riots
> and deal with their causes. Today I
> want to give the other side. There is
> certainly something painfully sad

about a riot. One sees screaming
youngsters and angry adults fighting
hopelessly and aimlessly against impossible odds. And deep down within
them, you can see a desire for self-
destruction, a kind of suicidal longing.[97]

He added that in none of the cities in which
riots had occurred had there been any of
the concrete improvements that had followed the organized, nonviolent demonstrations of the civil rights movement.

Years before the riots, King had
warned that the use of violence would cost
the movement the support of compassionate people. His prediction proved accu-
rate. An article printed in 1968, three
summers after the Watts riot and eight
days after its author's assassination, contained King's assertion that riots did nothing to improve race relations. He said that
not only did riots increase fear of blacks
among white people, it also made them
feel that racial prejudice against violent,
destructive people was justified. But King
also recognized that as people worried
that the violence would increase to uncon-
trollable levels, little was being done to improve the conditions the rioters were
protesting. He warned:

> But I'm convinced that if something
> isn't done to deal with the very harsh
> and real economic problems of the
> ghetto, the talk of guerrilla warfare is
> going to become much more real. The
> nation has not yet recognized the seri-
> ousness of it. Congress hasn't been
> willing to do anything about it. . . . As
> committed as I am to nonviolence, I
> have to face this fact: if we do not get a
> positive response in Washington, many
> more Negroes will begin to think and
> act in violent terms.[98]

Taking It to the North

Martin Luther King Jr. and his supporters believed that one way to solve the problems faced by black people in inner cities and to stop the violence was to reorganize the civil rights movement. The Watts riot showed civil rights activists that though African Americans had advanced tremendously in ten years, gaining political, social, and economic power, it wasn't enough to fight for laws for equal treatment of blacks as U.S. citizens. It was also necessary to understand that there were two groups of African Americans: those who were prospering and could readily benefit from the civil rights laws, and those who were mired in the economic and social problems of the inner cities of the country, for whom new laws did little. A statement by the National Committee of Negro Churchmen that appeared in the November 6, 1966, *New York Times* reflects the movement's perception of the conditions affecting the response of black people who lived in ghettos:

> Is it conceivable that the shrill cry "Burn, Baby, Burn" in Watts, Los Angeles, and across this country, could ever be invented by men with reasonable chance to make a living, to live in a decent neighborhood, to get an adequate education for their children? Is it conceivable that men with reasonable prospects for life, liberty, and the pursuit of happiness for themselves and for their children could ever put the torch to their own streets? The answer is obvious. These are the anguished, desperate acts of men, women, and children who have been taught to hate themselves and who have been herded and confined like cattle in rat-infested slums.[99]

In an effort to change the ghetto conditions, the civil rights movement began to focus less on the South, where desegregation was taking place, and more on

Victims of Negro Hostility

In a 1966 article excerpted in A Documentary History of the Negro People in the United States, *Martin Luther King Jr. indicates that whites should not interpret the riots as threatening.*

"I can only conclude that the Negro, even in his bitterest moments, is not intent on killing white men to be free. This does not mean that the Negro is a saint who abhors violence. Unfortunately, a check of the hospitals in any Negro community on any Saturday night will make you painfully aware of the violence within the Negro community. Hundreds of victims of shooting and cutting lie bleeding in the emergency rooms, but there is seldom if ever a white person who is the victim of Negro hostility."

cities far from the old Civil War battle-fields, where segregation of blacks into communities like Watts was an accepted practice. The first target city was Chicago, where one million African Americans lived in ghettos. Shortly before his death, King had begun to speak about shifting from a civil rights movement focused on laws to a human rights movement that would concentrate on improving employment and housing conditions for African Americans. In a November 1965 article called "Next Step the North," he expressed this new emphasis:

> Civil rights leaders had long thought that the North would benefit derivatively from [as a result of] the southern struggle. They assumed that without massive upheavals certain systematic changes were inevitable as the whole nation reexamined and searched its conscience. This was a miscalculation. It was founded on the belief that opposition in the North was not intransigent [stubbornly refusing to change]; that it was flexible and was, if not fully, at least partially hospitable to corrective influences. We forgot what we knew daily in the South—freedom is not given, it is won by struggle.[100]

A Campaign for Improvement

The movement campaigned to improve jobs and income, which were considered the most crucial concerns for African Americans. King proposed an economic bill of rights to guarantee jobs to people of all races who were willing and able to work, and an income for those who could

Martin Luther King Jr. argued that changing laws to improve living conditions for African Americans was not enough; he advocated a focus on human rights instead of civil rights.

not, because of age or disabilities. King said that a program that would provide jobs would minimize the number of riots. He did not suggest that such a plan would stop the violence, however. The campaign also included a call for more low-income housing and for improving ghetto schools. Such a campaign, King felt, would be an alternative way to confront the issues without destroying life or property. He also made it clear that the movement would not tolerate violence.

Another change made to the civil rights movement was a call for African Americans to help each other. In the ten-year period of civil rights advancement, a widening gulf had developed in the black

A Defense of the Civil Rights Movement

Civil rights leaders were dealt a double blow after the Watts riot. Not only were they accused by some groups as having stirred up people's emotions until they burst out in uncontrolled anger, but they also had to come to terms with the failure of the movement in which they had worked so hard for ten years to make substantial improvements in the circumstances of inner-city blacks. In this excerpt from "Where Do We Go from Here?", reprinted in A Documentary History of the Negro People in the United States, *edited by Herbert Aptheker, Martin Luther King Jr. defends the movement and denounces the use of riots as a means to effect social change.*

"Occasionally Negroes contend that the 1965 Watts riot and the other riots in various cities represented effective civil rights action. But those who express this view always end up with stumbling words when asked what concrete gains have been won as a result. At best, the riots have produced a little additional antipoverty money allotted by frightened government officials, and a few water-sprinklers to cool the children of the ghettoes. It is something like improving the food in the prison while the people remain securely incarcerated behind bars. Nowhere have the riots won any concrete improvement such as have the organized protest demonstrations.

It is perfectly clear that a violent revolution on the part of American blacks would find no sympathy and support from the white population and very little from the majority of Negroes themselves."

Martin Luther King Jr. supported nonviolent demonstrations to create effective change for black people.

community between the middle class and the poor. As desegregation helped to improve the lives of many African Americans, some experts claimed that those who moved up lost interest in continuing to foster the movement. The black psychologist Kenneth B. Clark attributed this attitude to an unwillingness to make personal sacrifices beyond those already required by African-American life itself.

Warning that African Americans had to work together without the use of violence, the NAACP's Roy Wilkins wrote: "We will have ghetto upheavals until the Negro community itself, through the channels that societies have fashioned since tribal beginnings, takes firm charge of its destiny. Not its destiny vis-à-vis a cop on the beat, but its destiny in the world of adults."[101]

The Movement Falls Apart

But even with the new focus of the civil rights movement, there was no immediate cure to the problems of the ghetto. The assassination of King in 1968 left the civil rights movement in turmoil. That year the Kerner Commission, appointed by President Johnson to study race relations, found the country deeply divided by color. The commission also found that blacks did not have the same opportunities as whites in education, employment, or housing, and were living far below the economic standard of the majority, as well. These were all issues present three years before in Watts. Nonetheless, the presidential report had a profound effect on the development of programs to fight poverty and improve job training and education for African Americans. The civil

Roy Wilkins, executive director of the NAACP, encouraged the black community to take charge of its own destiny in a nonviolent manner.

rights movement fought for a final piece of legislation, the Civil Rights Act of 1968, which prohibits racial discrimination in the sale or rental of housing. With this law it became illegal to attempt to prevent African Americans or members of any other ethnic minority group from moving into any neighborhood in which they can secure housing.

After King's death, the civil rights movement continued to experience the division and decline that had begun in King's last years. As a result of the Voting Rights Act, in 1966 black leaders were elected in the South for the first time. In 1967 Carl B. Stokes of Cleveland, Ohio, became the first black mayor of a major city. Increasingly, affirmative action programs, made legal by the 1964 Civil Rights Act as a means of obtaining employment for qualified people who might otherwise have been victimized by discriminatory hiring practices, helped African Americans secure good jobs. The goals of the civil rights movement before Watts had helped to move many African Americans away from segregation and out of the ghettos.

As the decade ended, groups like the Black Panthers disbanded because of a lack of leadership. Rioting also had run its course, partially because by then, in the ghettos of the country's major cities, there was little property left to destroy. Rather, angry residents faced empty lots and demolished buildings.

Kindling for Another Riot

But perhaps the main reason for the abandonment of rioting as a means of social protest was that it did not work. As King had said, no major gains had been realized for African Americans who rioted. While some inner-city residents valued the recognition they had gained through rioting, historian Lewis Lansky says that in every case,

A police officer directs Watts riot refugees to a shelter. One reason rioting declined by the end of the 1960s was that there was not much property left to destroy in many ghettos.

Preparation for the Next Time

The conclusion of an FBI manual entitled Prevention and Control of Mobs and Riots, *excerpted in* Burn, Baby, Burn *by Jerry Cohen and William S. Murphy, contains a somber evaluation of the aftermath of a riot and the possibility of a recurrence.*

"The exercise of violence during a riot does not result in a purification of the atmosphere, leading to peace. It is not a situation in which excess energy is worked off, leaving the decks cleared for cooperation. Deep scars are left on both sides through this failure of law enforcement to control people. The rioters, especially the more active ones, take pride in their accomplishments regardless of the outcome of the riot. They do not feel guilty and tend to justify their actions on the basis of 'Moral reasons.' One of the immediate consequences of a riot is a stimulation of determination to prepare for the 'next time.' Far from eliminating the differences which caused the violence in the first place, they are consolidated, reinforced and deepened."

the riots did more harm than good: "Conditions after the riots were actually worse. You had neighborhoods that had had lively businesses turn into streets of boarded-up buildings. The riots destroyed an already poor economy in the ghettos."[102]

Even today, there has been little rebuilding in riot-ruined ghettos. In most cases, banks will not give mortgages to applicants who want to start a business in these neighborhoods because such an investment is considered a high risk for riot damage. Economic opportunities have not improved either, as factories that once offered jobs to unskilled workers close up, increasing unemployment.

The problems of inner-city black America persist. No matter what the advancements in race relations or the improvements in quality of life for many African Americans, those who are poor almost uniformly remain poor. Today drugs, AIDS, gang wars, and teen pregnancy increase the problems in inner-city populations, which are no longer populated only by African Americans, but by poor Hispanics and Asians as well. In over thirty years of civil rights progress, the conditions in communities like Watts have not been improved. The kindling for another riot is always smoldering, and society has not yet figured out how to extinguish it.

Watts Today

For a time after the ashes of the Watts riot settled over the community, the area experienced a renaissance, a rebirth. There were programs for job training, economic development, social reform, and artistic expression. Television camera operators were trained, black dolls manufactured, plays produced, a movie theater opened, and small industry developed, including a factory that produced big-league "Watts Walloper" baseball bats. A new community center was built. New businesses came in and some old businesses were rebuilt. Cultural events were scheduled and job training was made available within the community.

The Watts Labor Community Action Committee, formed in the wake of the riot, developed over the years a steady stream of low-income housing units, job programs, youth activities, and programs for senior citizens. The organization built houses in the neighborhood and ran a homeless shelter and a housing project for seniors.

Said James Taylor, a Watts resident who was director of a performing arts group called Mafundi Institute:

> You just cannot imagine how exciting it was. Everyone was coming down here, holding classes, helping, check-ing it out. We built our own building with our own stage. Instead of hanging out on the streets, kids would come here after school to take part in what we were doing or just hang out.[103]

A New Mayor

During the next decade, there were changes in Los Angeles' political administration as well. In 1973 a black mayor, Thomas Bradley, replaced Samuel Yorty. Under Bradley's leadership, racial tensions in the city were calmed. More African Americans, as well as Hispanics and Asians, were elected to political office, and more and more African Americans were added to the Los Angeles Police Department, which today has a black chief, Willie L. Williams. Bradley was also credited with inspiring the return of many markets, shops, record stores, and drugstores that had been driven from the area by the 1965 fires. One of Bradley's main efforts, the restoration of a shopping district to Watts, culminated in the opening of a shopping center in 1984. This was extremely helpful for residents who had had to leave the area for their main shopping needs. The major accomplishment, however, was the opening in 1972 of the Martin Luther King Jr./Drew Medical Center, the first hospital in Watts.

But even with these achievements by people in the community, many of the goals of improving education, employment opportunities, and police relations, as outlined by the McCone Commission, remained unfulfilled. In fact, the construction of the new hospital was one of the only recommendations of the McCone Report that was carried out. Those in the African-American community old enough to recall the aftermath of the Watts riot remember the excitement the programs temporarily brought and the despair that later returned. Grace Payne, former director of the Westminster Neighborhood Association, organized in 1959, said that there had been a lot of media and government attention focused on the area, but it turned out not to have much effect. "Everybody was so concerned about Watts. They were going to do so much. They drew up all these plans. And then life went on."[104]

Looking back on the situation, a 1992 *Los Angeles Times* article reported, "The celebrities and other notables had stopped coming around, the donations had dried up, and some of the economic schemes had simply proved unworkable."[105]

Another Riot

A little over a quarter-century later, in April 1992, a second riot shattered South Central Los Angeles, just four miles northwest of Watts, leaving 51 dead, and 2,328 injured, with a cost to the city of at least $717 million in property damage. This riot, the worst in American history, was a thirty-six-hour binge of destruction that followed the determination by a California jury that four police officers who had been videotaped beating motorist Rodney G. King were not guilty of using excessive force. The scene in April and May was eerily familiar to the people of Watts, declares Tommy Jaquette, who had participated in

Thomas Bradley became mayor of Los Angeles in 1973. He worked to reestablish the shopping district of Watts and to open the first hospital in the area.

A View of Watts Today

"In some respects, there have been gains made. When we look at housing patterns, the city is probably less segregated than it was 30 years ago. There probably have been gains—I don't think substantial gains—in terms of the work force being more diversified in categories other than entry-level and what you might call traditional jobs held by minorities, particularly African-Americans. . . .

There was also none of the revitalization that was promised to rebuild South Central Los Angeles. If you drive through South Central Los Angeles now, you can still see the ravages of 30 years ago where there are still vacant lots and vacant tracts of land. If you remember 1965, all of those things were talked about—light industry, industrial parks, ways to revitalize."

McClain has this to say:

"In some respects we're better off and in some respects we're much worse off.

As far as some of the overt oppression, it was much worse then. Today, I think the problem is that the resources are dwindling. Now, it's who you know and what kind of influence you can exert in the bodies that are cutting up the money, like Congress and the Senate and so forth.

There's been no real leadership in the poor communities. Leadership that was there in the '60's right after the rebellion—or the riots, whichever you want to refer to it as—there was a lot of energy that came up and was either co-opted or beaten down over the last 30 years.

There's no real grass-roots leadership. There is a leadership of sorts, but it's in a fog. Young people are speaking out but [many] are drugged out, so their leadership is not in the way that it could be most beneficial or advantageous to the people that they're trying to lead."

the 1965 riot. On the first day of the 1992 riot, April 29, Jaquette went to see the crowds of angry teenagers gathered in Los Angeles. He told *Los Angeles Times* reporters that he remembered the excitement of being in the earlier riots. "I was in it from the first fire to the last fire. It felt real good." But twenty-seven years later, he watched for a while, and then drove away, noting for reporters: "I knew what those kids were going through. I felt the same way they did. . . . I knew the Establishment would have the upper hand at the end, that we would burn and sputter out. I just wanted to be out there to see it, to be a part of it."[106]

A New Commission

After the 1992 riot, as in 1965, a commission was formed to determine the cause of the disturbance. The Assembly Special Committee on the Los Angeles Crisis found itself restating the same conclusions the McCone Commission had made nearly three decades earlier. They found that the level of poverty and despair in South Central Los Angeles matched that of the 1960s. McCone had identified poverty, segregation, a lack of education and employment opportunities, widespread perceptions of

Burned-out buildings from the 1992 riot in Los Angeles are a startling reminder of the Watts riot decades earlier.

police abuse, and unequal consumer services as the principal complaints that fueled the 1965 riot. The report of the Assembly Special Committee on the Los Angeles Crisis stated that—though the 1992 rioters included many Hispanics and the lawbreakers' targets were now mostly prosperous Asian businesses—little had changed in Los Angeles since 1965. The report noted that reforms and recommendations made by the earlier panel had been mostly unfulfilled.

While the King trial may have ignited the riots, the tinder had been there long before 1992. Some spokespeople from South Central Los Angeles commented that the reaction of Los Angeles rioters showed that the basic problems of Watts had not been addressed. The anger was still there. Referring to those who regarded the Rodney King verdict as unfair, Cynthia Hamilton, a professor of Pan African studies at Cal State Los Angeles, said: "There were a lot of people who were dissatisfied with what they considered a miscarriage of justice. But when you look at the intensity of the response, both in and outside of Los Angeles, then we're talking about deep-seated ills that haven't been addressed."[107]

Looters raid a stereo store during the 1992 riot. Problems in South Central Los Angeles that remained since the 1965 riot fueled the riot in 1992.

"A Richer Place"

August 1995 was the thirtieth anniversary of the 1965 Watts riot. There had been some important changes to the area over the years. A mix of private and public monies had funded two shopping centers, a Metro Blue Line transit station, and the start of construction of a state-of-the-art library. In addition, the Watts Health Foundation operates a comprehensive health care center to improve the health of residents.

Grace Payne notes that many buildings were rebuilt after the 1965 riot and expresses hope that the damage from 1992 will be repaired faster:

> What was constructed as a result of the Watts rebellion is still standing: two new shopping centers; Martin Luther King, Jr., Hospital; the Watts Health Foundation; two banks; a post office; and a library. Homes and businesses that were lost this time will also be rebuilt, but I hope it's done soon—that we don't have to wait another 30 years.[108]

In 1995 Habitat for Humanity, an organization that helps people build inexpensive, quality homes, built thirty-one new single-family homes in the Watts community. The Watts Towers—sculptures known as one of the world's greatest examples of folk art, made by Italian immigrant Simon Rodia in 1919—attract thousands of visitors annually, bringing tourist dollars to local businesses. The Watts Labor Community Action Committee continues to provide job and skills training, subsidies to renters, and transportation services. The Inner City Cultural Center produces plays. Also, the community has a more diverse ethnic population.

Habitat for Humanity built thirty-one homes in Watts after the 1992 riot. Here, actor David Hyde-Pierce assists in the construction.

Mark Greenfield, executive director of the Watts Tower Arts Center, said, "I think we're richer as a city for the cultural diversity we have. Here, we've got a mix of everything. From that standpoint, it's made it a richer place."[109]

Unresolved Problems

But some areas of concern, despite slight improvements, are the same as those cited by the Watts residents of thirty years ago: namely, police-community relations,

Poor police-civilian relations were a factor in both the 1965 and 1992 riots. LAPD officers have recently begun efforts to improve the situation between police and the community of South Central Los Angeles.

education, and poverty. Since the 1992 riot, the Los Angeles Police Department has been making an effort to improve its relationship with the community. Rita Walters, a Los Angeles City Council member explains:

> Police-community relations are still uneven and downright problematic in some instances. Since '92 there is a new sensitivity, and officers and management that I interact with have been trying very hard to be responsive to the needs of the community while doing their job.[110]

Furthermore, while former mayor Bradley was able to claim vast improvements in housing and employment in the years following 1965, education continues to be one of the area's major problems. Bradley states, "I think the quality of education is going to remain one of our nagging problems, not just in Watts but all over the city of Los Angeles, until we revolutionize and reform the educational program in the city."[111]

Watts is still considered to be a poor area of Los Angeles. While many more people have been able to get good-paying jobs and move out of the community, those who have remained still struggle with low-wage work or no work at all.

Hope For the Future of Watts

But author Earl Ofari Hutchinson sees hope for the future of Watts in the hands of today's students. Each year, he says, professionals and businesspeople visit Markham Junior High School in Watts to talk about their work. Neat, clean-cut, respectful students fire eager questions at the speakers, seemingly full of hope for the future. Hutchinson described a modern Watts as a community that, while not perfect, has been able to survive:

> Watts can hardly be considered a paradise. It still ranks among the leaders in L.A. County in rates of gang violence, drug arrests, teen pregnancy, welfare dependency, and school dropouts. But Watts should no longer be considered America's symbol of urban violence and despair. Hope can rise from the ashes.[112]

The angry voices of the rioters during that hot summer week over thirty years ago were heard across the nation. But perhaps the voices of today's youth will ring not with anger but with expectations for the future in a community that has withstood the fires of rage.

Notes

Introduction: Image and Reality

1. James E. Jackson, "Watts Burns with Rage," in Herbert Aptheker, ed., *A Documentary History of the Negro People in the United States,* vol. 7. New York: Carol Publishing Group, 1994, p. 370.

2. Louie Robinson, "This Would Never Have Happened . . . If They Hadn't Kicked That Man," *Ebony,* October 1965, p. 114.

3. Quoted in Robinson, "This Would Never Have Happened . . . ," pp. 121–22.

4. Martin Luther King Jr., "Next Step the North," in Aptheker, *A Documentary History,* p. 387.

Chapter 1: A Decade of Progress

5. Quoted in Juan Williams, *Eyes on the Prize: America's Civil Rights Years, 1954–1965.* New York: Penguin Group, 1987, p. 34.

6. Williams, *Eyes on the Prize,* p. 38.

7. Williams, *Eyes on the Prize,* p. 122.

8. Quoted in Williams, *Eyes on the Prize,* p. 89.

9. Bayard Rustin, *Strategies for Freedom: The Changing Patterns of Black Protest.* New York: Columbia University Press, 1976, p. 37.

10. Rustin, *Strategies for Freedom,* p. 46.

11. Williams, *Eyes on the Prize,* p. 202.

12. Quoted in Williams, *Eyes on the Prize,* pp. 282–83.

13. Williams, *Eyes on the Prize,* pp. 286–87.

14. Rustin, *Strategies for Freedom,* p. 57.

15. Whitney M. Young Jr., "The Negro Revolt," in Aptheker, *A Documentary History,* p. 274.

Chapter 2: Port of Entry: Watts Before the Riot

16. Robert Kirsch, introduction to *Burn, Baby, Burn: The Los Angeles Race Riot, August, 1965,* by Jerry Cohen and William S. Murphy. New York: E. P. Dutton, 1966, p. 13.

17. Paul Bullock, ed., *Watts: The Aftermath, An Inside View of the Ghetto by the People of Watts.* New York: Grove Press, 1969, p. 14.

18. Bullock, *Watts: The Aftermath,* pp. 18–19.

19. King, "Next Step the North," in Aptheker, *A Documentary History,* p. 391.

20. Bullock, *Watts: The Aftermath,* p. 19.

21. Quoted in Bullock, *Watts: The Aftermath,* p. 24.

22. A Report by the Governor's Commission on the Los Angeles Riots, "Violence in the City: An End or a Beginning?" in Robert M. Fogelson, ed., *Mass Violence in America: The Los Angeles Riots.* New York: Arno Press, 1969, p. 90.

Chapter 3: The Arrests That Triggered the Riot

23. Bullock, *Watts: The Aftermath,* p. 135.

24. Quoted in Robinson "This Would Never Have Happened . . . ," p. 120.

25. Robinson, "This Would Never Have Happened . . . ," p. 120.

26. David O. Sears and John B. McConahay, *The Politics of Violence: The New Urban Blacks and the Watts Riot.* Boston: Houghton Mifflin, 1973, p. 4.

27. Quoted in Robinson, "This Would Never Have Happened . . . ," p. 116.

28. Quoted in Cohen and Murphy, *Burn, Baby, Burn,* p. 34.

29. Cohen and Murphy, *Burn, Baby, Burn,* p. 36.

30. Cohen and Murphy, *Burn, Baby, Burn,* p. 36.

31. Quoted in Robinson, "This Would Never Have Happened . . . ," pp. 116–17.

32. Quoted in Robinson, "This Would Never Have Happened . . . ," p. 117.

33. Quoted in Cohen and Murphy, *Burn, Baby, Burn,* p. 39.

34. Cohen and Murphy, *Burn, Baby, Burn,* p. 47.

35. Quoted in "Trigger of Hate," *Time,* August 20, 1965, p. 16.

36. Quoted in Robinson, "This Would Never Have Happened . . . ," p. 114.

37. Quoted in Robert Conot, *Rivers of Blood, Years of Darkness: The Unforgettable Classic Account of the Watts Riot.* New York: William Morrow, 1968, p. 17.

38. Quoted in Conot, *Rivers of Blood, Years of Darkness,* p. 18.

39. Quoted in Conot, *Rivers of Blood, Years of Darkness,* p. 18.

40. Quoted in Conot, *Rivers of Blood, Years of Darkness,* p. 19.

41. Conot, *Rivers of Blood, Years of Darkness,* p. 20.

42. Quoted in Conot, *Rivers of Blood, Years of Darkness,* p. 20.

43. Cohen and Murphy, *Burn, Baby, Burn,* pp. 57–58.

44. Conot, *Rivers of Blood, Years of Darkness,* p. 29.

Chapter 4: Burn, Baby, Burn!

45. Cohen and Murphy, *Burn, Baby, Burn,* p. 65.

46. Cohen and Murphy, *Burn, Baby, Burn,* p. 67.

47. Quoted in Cohen and Murphy, *Burn, Baby, Burn,* p. 68.

48. Quoted in "Trigger of Hate," p. 16.

49. Quoted in Cohen and Murphy, *Burn, Baby, Burn,* p. 76.

50. Quoted in Cohen and Murphy, *Burn, Baby, Burn,* p. 87.

51. Quoted in "Trigger of Hate," p. 16.

52. Quoted in Cohen and Murphy, *Burn, Baby, Burn,* p. 97.

53. Quoted in "End of a 'Quiet Summer'—A Flare-Up of Riots," *U.S. News & World Report,* August 23, 1965, p. 6.

Chapter 5: The Spread of Destruction

54. Quoted in Cohen and Murphy, *Burn, Baby, Burn,* p. 106.

55. Quoted in Cohen and Murphy, *Burn, Baby, Burn,* p. 126.

56. "Trigger of Hate," p. 17.

57. Cohen and Murphy, *Burn, Baby, Burn,* p. 188.

58. Quoted in Cohen and Murphy, *Burn, Baby, Burn,* p. 183.

59. Quoted in "Trigger of Hate," p. 17.

60. Quoted in Cohen and Murphy, *Burn, Baby, Burn,* p. 134.

61. David Reed, interview with author, October 1995.

62. Quoted in Cohen and Murphy, *Burn, Baby, Burn,* p. 183.

63. Quoted in Cohen and Murphy, *Burn, Baby, Burn*, p. 185.

64. Quoted in Cohen and Murphy, *Burn, Baby, Burn*, p. 185.

65. Quoted in Cohen and Murphy, *Burn, Baby, Burn*, p. 184.

66. Cohen and Murphy, *Burn, Baby, Burn*, p. 194.

67. Quoted in Cohen and Murphy, *Burn, Baby, Burn*, p. 251.

68. Cohen and Murphy, *Burn, Baby, Burn*, p. 228.

Chapter 6: Charcoal Alley: The Immediate Aftermath

69. "After the Bloodbath," *Newsweek*, August 30, 1965, p. 15.

70. Robert M. Fogelson, ed., *Mass Violence in America: The Los Angeles Riots*. New York: Arno Press, 1969, p. 25.

71. Quoted in Conot, *Rivers of Blood, Years of Darkness*, p. 390.

72. Quoted in James E. Jackson, "Watts Burns with Rage," in Aptheker, *A Documentary History*, p. 370.

73. Quoted in Jackson, "Watts Burns with Rage," in Aptheker, *A Documentary History*, pp. 371–72.

74. Quoted in *Eyes on the Prize: America at the Racial Crossroads, 1965–1985*. Boston: Blackside, 1990. Program 2: "Two Societies (1965–1968)."

75. Quoted in "After the Bloodbath," p. 15.

76. Quoted in "After the Bloodbath," p. 15.

77. Robert Blauner, "Whitewash Over Watts: The Failure of the McCone Commission Report," in Fogelson, *Mass Violence in America*, p. 182.

78. "The Negro After Watts," *Time*, August 27, 1965, p. 16.

79. Quoted in Conot, *Rivers of Blood, Years of Darkness*, p. 456.

80. Quoted in Jackson, "Watts Burns with Rage," in Aptheker, *A Documentary History*, p. 372.

Chapter 7: Why Did It Happen? A Search for Answers

81. "The Loneliest Road," *Time*, August 27, 1965, p. 10.

82. "After the Bloodbath," p. 18.

83. Don Moser, "There's No Easy Place to Pin the Blame," *Life*, August 27, 1965, pp. 24–25.

84. Quoted in "The Tough Cop of L.A.," *Newsweek*, August 30, 1965, p. 17.

85. Quoted in "The Loneliest Road," p. 11.

86. "After the Bloodbath," p. 18.

87. The Governor's Commission, "Violence in the City," in Fogelson, *Mass Violence in America*, pp. 7–8.

88. The Governor's Commission, "Violence in the City," in Fogelson, *Mass Violence in America*, pp. 4–5.

89. The Governor's Commission, "Violence in the City," in Fogelson, *Mass Violence in America*, p. 35.

90. Quoted in Henry Weinstein, "Few of McCone Panel's Ideas Were Carried Out," *Los Angeles Times*, May 11, 1992, p. A8.

91. Weinstein, "Few of McCone Panel's Ideas Were Carried Out," p. A8.

92. Blauner, "Whitewash Over Watts," in Fogelson, *Mass Violence in America*, p. 169.

93. The Governor's Commission, "Violence in the City," in Fogelson, *Mass Violence in America*, p. 93.

94. Quoted in Weinstein, "Few of McCone Panel's Ideas Were Carried Out," p. A14.

95. Bayard Rustin, "The Watts 'Manifesto' and the McCone Report," in Fogelson, *Mass Violence in America*, p. 161.

Chapter 8: The Legacy of Watts

96. Martin Luther King Jr., "Nonviolence: The Only Road to Freedom," in Aptheker, *A Documentary History*, p. 447.

97. Martin Luther King Jr., "Where Do We Go from Here?" in Aptheker, *A Documentary History*, p. 523.

98. Martin Luther King, Jr., "Showdown for Nonviolence," in Aptheker, *A Documentary History*, p. 552.

99. National Committee of Negro Churchmen, "Racism and the Elections: The American Dilemma, 1966," in Aptheker, *A Documentary History*, p. 456.

100. King, "Next Step the North," in Aptheker, *A Documentary History*, p. 389.

101. Quoted in "The Negro After Watts," *Time*, p. 17.

102. Lewis Lansky, Ph.D., interview with author, September 6, 1996.

Epilogue: Watts Today

103. Quoted in David Colker and Marc Lacey, "From Watts' 1965 Ashes: High Hopes, Heartaches," *Los Angeles Times*, May 10, 1992, p. A1.

104. Quoted in Colker and Lacey, "From Watts' 1965 Ashes," p. A20.

105. Colker and Lacey, "From Watts' 1965 Ashes," p. A1.

106. Quoted in Stephen Braun and Ron Russell, "Riots Are Violent Reruns for the Veterans of Watts," *Los Angeles Times*, May, 4, 1992, p. A11.

107. Quoted in Carla Rivera, "City Has Changed, but Not Roots of Unrest," *Los Angeles Times*, October 3, 1992, p. B1.

108. Quoted in Ken Wibecan, "Amazing Grace," *Modern Maturity*, August/September 1992, p. 14.

109. Mark Greenfield, Voices, "Piecemeal Gains but Little Direction," *Daily News*, August 13, 1995, p. 4.

110. Rita Walters, Voices, "Piecemeal Gains but Little Direction," p. 1.

111. Tom Bradley, Voices, "Piecemeal Gains but Little Direction," p. 1.

112. Earl Ofari Hutchinson, "Watts, 30 Years Later," *Daily News*, August 13, 1995, p. 1.

For Further Reading

Gregory Alan-Williams, *A Gathering of Heroes, Reflections on Rage and Responsibility, a Memoir of the Los Angeles Riots.* Chicago: Academy Chicago Publishers, 1994. The author is an actor who rescued a Japanese man who was being beaten during the 1992 Los Angeles riot. The book describes the sights and sounds of the riot.

Herbert Aptheker, *Afro-American History: The Modern Era.* New York: Carol Publishing Group, 1971. This fascinating account by an African-American historian of black history from 1900 to 1970 includes a chapter entitled "The Watts Ghetto Uprising."

Nathan Cohen, ed., *The Los Angeles Riots, a Socio-Psychological Study.* New York: Praeger, 1970. For readers who like numbers, this book provides statistics about who the participants and non-participants were in the 1965 Watts riot.

James D. Delk, *Fires & Furies, the L.A. Riots.* Palm Springs, CA: ETC Publications, 1995. A narrative that describes the 1992 Los Angeles riot in vivid detail.

William Dudley, ed., *The Civil Rights Movement.* San Diego: Greenhaven Press, 1996. A collection of essays that depicts the many controversies and points of view inherent in the civil rights movement, right up to the 1990s.

Anna Kosof, *The Civil Rights Movement and Its Legacy.* New York: Franklin Watts, 1989. A history of the civil rights movement and its effects on American society, with many interviews of participants.

Peter B. Levy, ed., *Documentary History of the Modern Civil Rights Movement.* New York: Greenwood Press, 1992. Contains essays by many participants in the civil rights movement; brings reader up to the 1980s.

Charles Patterson, *Social Reform Movements: The Civil Rights Movement.* New York: Facts On File, 1995. A thorough look at the black struggle for civil rights from slavery until modern times.

Fred Powledge, *We Shall Overcome: Heroes of the Civil Rights Movement.* New York: Charles Scribner's Sons, 1993. Interesting stories of people who joined the civil rights movement.

Videotape series, *Eyes on the Prize: America's Civil Rights Years (1954–1965)* and *Eyes on the Prize II: America at the Racial Crossroads (1965–mid 1980s).* Boston: Blackside. This fascinating videotape series brings the civil rights movement to life through film clips and interviews. "Program 2: Two Societies (1965–1968)" begins with the Watts riot and ends with the assassination of Martin Luther King Jr.

Works Consulted

"After the Bloodbath," *Newsweek*, August 30, 1965. A description of the riot and the mood of the country afterward.

Herbert Aptheker, ed., *A Documentary History of the Negro People in the United States*, vol. 7. New York: Carol Publishing Group, 1994. This collection of moving essays from civil rights leaders and historians gives an insider's perspective on the movement.

Bill Boyarsky, "Ashes of a Mayor's Dream," *Los Angeles Times*, May 1, 1992. An interview with Thomas Bradley, who had been the first black mayor of Los Angeles, after the 1992 riot in that city.

Stephen Braun and Ron Russell, "Riots Are Violent Reruns for the Veterans of Watts," *Los Angeles Times*, May 4, 1992. Compares the 1992 riot with the 1965 riot in the same area.

Paul Bullock, ed., *Watts: The Aftermath, An Inside View of the Ghetto by the People of Watts*. New York: Grove Press, 1969. Includes the historical background of the Watts community; chapters are broken down by issue and contain interviews with Watts residents.

Jerry Cohen and William S. Murphy, *Burn, Baby, Burn: The Los Angeles Race Riot, August, 1965*. New York: E. P. Dutton, 1966. A fast-paced and easy-to-read, day-by-day account of the Watts riot, told by two journalists who were there and later interviewed hundreds of participants.

David Colker and Marc Lacey, "From Watts' 1965 Ashes: High Hopes, Heartaches," *Los Angeles Times*, May 10, 1992. Describes some of the rebuilding that took place in Watts after the riot.

Robert Conot, *Rivers of Blood, Years of Darkness: The Unforgettable Classic Account of the Watts Riot*. New York: William Morrow, 1968. A very detailed story of the Watts riot; contains interviews of many of those involved in the event.

———, "When Watts' Lessons Are Forgotten," *Los Angeles Times*, May 3, 1992. The author of a detailed account of the 1965 riot expresses dismay that the community has seemingly forgotten the repercussions of the event.

"End of a 'Quiet Summer'—A Flare-Up of Riots," *U.S. News & World Report*, August 23, 1965. A news report.

Eyes on the Prize: America at the Racial Crossroads, 1965–1985. Boston: Blackside, 1990. Program 2: "Two Societies (1965–1968)." A video that contains clips of the Watts riot and Martin Luther King Jr.'s response to the violence.

Robert M. Fogelson, ed., *Mass Violence in America: The Los Angeles Riots*. New York: Arno Press, 1969. A collection of works that includes the entire McCone Commission report, "Violence in the City: An End or a Beginning?" as well as essays by Fogelson, Bayard Rustin, and Robert Blauner, who critiqued the report.

V. P. Franklin, *Black Self-Determination*. Brooklyn: Lawrence Hill Books, 1992. A cultural history of the African-American civil rights movement.

Earl Ofari Hutchinson, "Watts, 30 Years Later," *Daily News*, August 13, 1995. An editorial, offering hope for Watts on the thirtieth anniversary of the 1965 riot.

Marc Lacey, "Victims of Riots Honored," *Los Angeles Times*, August 13, 1992. Discusses a Watts summer festival honoring the memory of people killed in the 1965 and 1992 riots.

"The Loneliest Road," *Time*, August 27, 1965. Los Angeles officials try to place the blame for the riot on one another.

Don Moser, "There's No Easy Place to Pin the Blame," *Life*, August 27, 1965. Police Chief William H. Parker speaks out against those who blame him for the riot.

"The Negro After Watts," *Time*, August 27, 1965. An essay that shows the mood of Watts after the riots.

"Police 'Brutality'—Fact or Fiction?" *U.S. News & World Report*, September 6, 1965. An examination of the issue of police brutality in inner cities.

Carla Rivera, "City Has Changed, but Not Roots of Unrest," *Los Angeles Times*, October 3, 1992. The Assembly Special Committee report on the 1992 riot.

———, "Riots' Causes Same as in '60s, State Panel Says," *Los Angeles Times*, October 2, 1992. The Assembly Special Committee on the 1992 riot determines that the causes of the riot are the same as those of 1965.

Louie Robinson, "This Would Never Have Happened . . . If They Hadn't Kicked That Man," *Ebony*, October 1965. The author met with the man who was kicked, Marquette Frye, and his brother, Ronald, and their mother, Rena, to hear the family's version of the story.

Bayard Rustin, *Strategies for Freedom: The Changing Patterns of Black Protest*. New York: Columbia University Press, 1976. Describes the stages of the civil rights movement; the chapter called "The Protest Era" attempts to explain why the Watts riot took place.

David O. Sears and John B. McConahay, *The Politics of Violence: The New Urban Blacks and the Watts Riot*. Boston: Houghton Mifflin, 1973. A study of the riot and why it took place.

"Shifting Patterns in Race Problem," *U.S. News & World Report*, August 23, 1965. Discusses the direction that black civil rights activists will take in the wake of the riot.

"The Tough Cop of L.A.," *Newsweek*, August 30, 1965. A collection of quotes by William H. Parker, the outspoken police chief, whose remarks are sometimes offensive.

"Trigger of Hate," *Time*, August 20, 1965. A day-by-day description of the Watts riot.

"Troubled Los Angeles—Race Is Only One of Its Problems," *U.S. News &*

World Report, August 30, 1965. A look at problems Los Angeles was facing in 1965, from pollution to the riots.

Voices, "Piecemeal Gains but Little Direction," *Daily News*, August 13, 1995. A collection of interviews with activists in Watts, who offer a rather dismal view of the modern conditions there.

Henry Weinstein, "Few of McCone Panel's Ideas Were Carried Out," *Los Angeles Times*, May 11, 1992. Examines recommendations the 1965 McCone Commission made that had not been carried out.

"Why Negroes Rioted in Watts—Official Report," *U.S. News & World Report*, December 20, 1965. A report of the McCone Commission's findings.

Ken Wibecan, "Amazing Grace," *Modern Maturity*, August/September 1992. An interview with Grace Payne, former director of the Westminster Neighborhood Center, an organization that tries to improve the lives of Watts residents.

Juan Williams, *Eyes on the Prize: America's Civil Rights Years, 1954-1965*. New York: Penguin Group, 1987. A companion to the video series, this book offers an easy-to-read guide to the civil rights movement just up to the Watts riot.

Index

Picture Credits

About the Author

Liza N. Burby is the author of two other books for Lucent Books, *World Hunger*, which is a 1996 New York Public Library Books for the Teen Age selection, and *Family Violence*. She is also the author of eighteen biographies for young readers. Burby also writes for the *New York Times, Newsday*, and national magazines, and is a frequent speaker on the topic of domestic violence.